Also by EDNA LEWIS

The Edna Lewis Cookbook

In Pursuit of Flavor

The Gift of Southern Cooking
(with Scott Peacock)

The Taste of Country Cooking

The Taste of
Country Cooking

EDNA LEWIS

Alfred A. Knopf   New York   2007

THIS IS A BORZOI BOOK
PUBLISHED BY ALFRED A. KNOPF

Copyright © 1976 by Edna Lewis
Preface copyright © 2006 by Judith B. Jones
Foreword copyright © 2006 by Alice Waters

www.aaknopf.com

Knopf, Borzoi Books, and the colophon are
registered trademarks of Random House, Inc.

The illustration *Bird on Nest* appears here with
the permission of the illustrator, Clare Leighton.

Haystacks by Thomas Nason
Great Apples by Moishe Smith
Winter Twilight by J. J. Lankes
appear courtesy of Associated American Artists

Portions of the Spring section appeared in
the May 1976 issue of *Gourmet*.

Library of Congress Cataloging-in-Publication Data
Lewis, Edna.
The taste of country cooking.
Includes index.
1. Cookery, American—Virginia. 2. Freetown, Va.—History. I. Title
TX715.L6684   641.5'975   75-36804
ISBN 0-307-26560-9

Manufactured in the United States of America
Originally published May 28, 1976
Thirtieth Anniversary Edition Published, August 1, 2006
Reprinted One Time
Third Printing, March 2007

*This book is dedicated to the memory of
the people of Freetown*

*and to Judith B. Jones, with many thanks
for her deep understanding.*

 # CONTENTS

Spring

Summer

Fall

Winter

APPENDIX & INDEX

FOREWORD

by Alice Waters

Miss Edna Regina Lewis was born in Virginia in 1916, in a bucolic, out-of-the-way settlement known as Freetown, which had been founded by her grandfather and other freed slaves after the emancipation of 1865. She enjoyed a childhood that could only be described as idyllic, in which the never-ending hard work of farming and cooking both sustained and entertained an entire community. In 1976, with the publication of this lovely, indispensable classic of a cookbook, she brought her lost paradise of Freetown back to life. Thanks to this book, a new generation was introduced to the glories of an American tradition worthy of comparison to the most evolved cuisines on earth, a tradition of simplicity and purity and sheer deliciousness that is only possible when food tastes like what it is, from a particular place, at a particular point in time.

To her readers thirty years ago, the community she depicted in these pages may have seemed even more remote than it does today. Back then, the possibility that many Americans might once again strive to eat only local, seasonal foods, raised or gathered or hooked by people they knew, seemed distant, at best. Back then, most of us were more or less resigned to the industrialization of our food, the mechanization of our work, the trivialization of our play, and the atomization of our communities. But with her recipes and reminiscences, Miss Lewis was able to gently suggest another way of being, one on a human scale, in harmony with the seasons and with our fellow man. For her, always, as it had in her childhood, pleasure flowed unstoppably out of *doing*. She saw clearly that the store-bought cake never brings lasting satisfaction; true contentment comes from baking it yourself, by hand, for someone you love. She also saw no need to rail against the absurdities of modernity; rather, she demonstrated the beauty of tradition, and by doing so, helped stir up a great longing for authenticity, accountability, and sustainability.

Another notable advocate of simplicity, Mahatma Gandhi, famously remarked that we must become the change we want to make in the world. Like Gandhi, Miss Lewis was as radical as she was traditional. To become the change she wanted to make, she left the racially divided South and plunged into the maelstrom of New York City, working variously as a type-setter for the *Daily Worker* and as a dressmaker for Marilyn Monroe, among other jobs, before she became the chef of an East Side restaurant in Manhattan called Café Nicholson and, later, of Gage & Tollner in Brooklyn. In between, for a time she had a pheasant farm, which she ran with the same hands-on delight and concentration with which she cooked. She never rejected her cultural heritage; she expanded on it. She loved to wear colorful West African–inspired dresses of her own design, and her devotion to the foodways of her childhood ultimately led her to found the Society for the Revival and Preservation of Southern Food. Her key insight was to recognize that truly great traditions belong to all the living, regardless of individual heritage; and that they belong to elective families as well as to those bound by consanguinity.

In the community of culinary celebrities, Miss Lewis's quiet dignity was legendary. On several occasions, my Chez Panisse crew and I traveled east to the big Meals on Wheels benefit in New York. Miss Lewis was unique among the high-powered chefs who were invited to cook at these affairs. Some of them would arrive with their food already made; some would arrive with big staffs and set up ruthlessly efficient production lines. Meanwhile, Miss Lewis would have set up all by herself in a little corner, and would be baking pies, one at a time, alone, or maybe with her friend Scott Peacock. There she would stand, a pillar of strength and calm, rolling out pie crust with a wooden rolling pin and crimping the pastry with her long, efficient fingers. She knew that real food made by hand means more to both those who make it and those who eat it. And she poured her self into her work because she knew that all you can take from this life is what you give away.

As you will discover from this book, Edna Lewis had an irresistible generosity and honesty of spirit. She was far more than the doyenne of Southern cooking. She was, and she remains, an inspiration to all of us who are striving to protect both biodiversity and cultural diversity by cooking real food in season and honoring our heritage through the ritual of the table. By holding on to her values and expressing them in her life's work, she set a shining example of how to bring beauty and meaning to everyday life.

PREFACE

by Judith Jones, Edna Lewis's editor at Knopf

It was in the spring of 1972 that I first met Edna Lewis. Bob Bernstein, the head of Random House at the time, had suggested to his friend Evangeline Peterson that she and Edna talk with me about the cookbook they were doing together.

I was immediately struck by Edna's regal presence when she walked into my office. She was wearing one of the African-style outfits that she had made herself—a colorful, long, batik skirt and top, with matching scarf draped loosely around her neck and dangling earrings that swung when she tossed back her head. I became even more entranced when she started talking about the foods of her childhood and how she had grown up in Freetown, Virginia, a farming community that her grandfather, a freed slave, had founded. Her face would light up as she recalled gathering wild asparagus along the fence row or of the many dishes her mother would prepare for Revival Sunday (and the long, agonizing wait to taste them). I sensed immediately from her pleasure in these memories that she must be a wonderful cook.

The book that she and Peterson had put together was based on the dishes Edna served at Café Nicholson, in Manhattan's East Fifties, where Truman Capote and Tennessee Williams and other artists and writers would congregate of an evening to taste real Southern food. But it was just a collection of those recipes along with what seemed like popular café fare. And anyway this book, called *The Edna Lewis Cookbook,* was already completed and on its way to the printer, so I could be of little help.

But the book I'd like to see, I said, would be made up of the kind of memories she had just described and of the ways in which she and her family and the people of Freetown raised their food and prepared it throughout the year. Would they give that a try?

They were excited at the prospect. But when they came back a few weeks later with some sample pages in hand, I was disappointed. "This isn't you, Edna," I said. "It isn't the voice I heard when you were talking to me." At that point Evangeline Peterson, to her great credit, withdrew, saying that yes, Edna should be writing the book herself.

The challenge now was to help Edna recover that voice, and I sensed that she was uneasy about going it alone. So we tried talking out a section one afternoon, with me asking questions and prodding for more detail, and then while we were still giddy with her total recall, I suggested she go straight home and put it all down just as she had told it to me. It worked miraculously. The next week she brought in several pages, handwritten on a long, yellow legal pad, and the words flowed. We repeated these sessions every week through that winter, and before long this book had taken shape.

I think that every reader will feel genuinely grateful for the memories Edna shares with us and for the many things she teaches us, from the proper way to fry chicken to the secret of making "flannel soft" biscuits. Thank you, Edna Lewis. You will always be with us in the pages of *The Taste of Country Cooking.*

ACKNOWLEDGMENTS

I wish to thank my sister, Mrs. Virginia Ellis, for her invaluable help and very fine recipes, and for spending many hours over the hot stove cooking, canning, and preserving to refresh our memories; and to thank my brother, Lue Stanley, for his devotion to my efforts and his love for Freetown. To Dr. Glen R. Thomas my sincere thanks for generously placing his home and garden at my disposal.

My appreciation also to Mrs. Grace Saran, a young organic enthusiast and an expert in the knowledge of edible wild mushrooms.

I want to especially thank my niece, Nina Williams, whose help was most important in typing and re-typing the manuscript. She has been working with me on this project for four years, beginning at the age of twelve.

INTRODUCTION

I grew up in Freetown, Virginia, a community of farming people. It wasn't really a town. The name was adopted because the first residents had all been freed from chattel slavery and they wanted to be known as a town of Free People. My grandfather had been one of the first: His family, along with two others, were granted land by a plantation owner, Claiborn R. Mason, Jr., for whom one of them had served as coachman. The property was situated just behind Lahore —a village consisting of only one post office and a general store built around 1840; it still stands today, looking very much the same as it did then.

After the first three families were settled, eight more joined in and purchased land. They built their houses in a circle around my grandfather's, which was in the center. My grandmother had been a brickmason as a slave—purchased for the sum of $950 by a rich landowner who had several tracts of land and wanted to build two imposing houses on different locations. Grandmother was put to work molding the bricks, then carrying them and laying them (one of the houses she worked on still stands today, owned and restored by a college professor, but the other was destroyed in the Civil War). It was a job that caused my grandmother great anguish because she would have to go off all day to work on the big house, leaving her babies in their cribs and not returning until late in the evening to feed and care for them. The fact that years later, after her children had grown up and were living in Freetown, she would still take her kerosene lamp and go upstairs to make sure they were there and all right is a measure of the pain she bore. It is no wonder that they decided to build a big house so they could all be together. The first part was made of logs, then they added four rooms and clapboarded the whole building. The kitchen was separated from the main house, as were all the kitchens in Freetown then.

The first school in the area was held in my grandfather's living room, chosen no doubt because he was one of the oldest in the community and had a large and lively family. Children came from as much as six or eight miles to learn, and the teacher was from Ohio, a graduate of Oberlin College. Soon Freetown became a lively place, with poetry readings, singing quartets, and productions of plays put on by the young people. One of the biggest achievements was when my youngest aunt went away to a boarding school at Manassas, Virginia; her brothers had all worked and raised the money to send her. Later my sisters, brothers, and I attended the first accredited school in the area, which was built with funds raised by the same teacher— then quite well along in years—who had taught in Grandfather's living room. And it was the early freedmen who built the church and the entertainment hall and organized events like Revival Week, Emancipation Day, and various other feasts that punctuated our farm year.

The spirit of pride in community and of cooperation in the work of farming is what made Freetown a very wonderful place to grow up in. Ours was a large family: my parents, my grandfather, three sisters, two brothers, and cousins who stayed with us from time to time, all living under the same roof. The farm was demanding but everyone shared in the work—tending the animals, gardening, harvesting, preserving the harvest, and, every day, preparing delicious foods that seemed to celebrate the good things of each season. As well, there was the bounty yielded up by the woods, fields, and streams. It was always fun to go searching for nuts and berries, to have the men bring in some game in the fall or the first fish of spring, all of which not only added to our regular supply of food but always brought something festive to the table.

Whenever there were major tasks on the farm, work that had to be accomplished quickly (and timing is so important in farming), then everyone pitched in, not just family but neighbors as well. And afterward we would all take part in the celebrations, sharing the rewards that follow hard labor. The year seemed to be broken up by great events such as hog butchering, Christmas, the cutting of ice in winter, springtime with its gathering of the first green vegetables and the stock going away to summer pasture, the dramatic moment of wheat threshing, the excitement of Revival Week, Race Day, and the observance of Emancipation Day. All these events were shared by the whole community, young and old alike. I guess that is why I have always felt that the people of Freetown were very special. They showed such love and affection for us as children, at the same time asking something of us, and they knew how to help each other so that the land would thrive for all. Each family had its own different talents, its special humor, but they were bound together in an important way.

Over the years since I left home and lived in different cities, I have kept thinking about the people I grew up with and about our way of life. Whenever I go back to visit my sisters and brothers, we relive old times, remembering the past. And when we share again in gathering wild strawberries, canning, rendering lard, finding walnuts, picking persimmons, making fruitcake, I realize how much the bond that held us had to do with food. Since we are the last of the original families, with no children to remember and carry on, I decided that I wanted to write down just exactly how we did things when I was growing up in Freetown that seemed to make life so rewarding. Although the founders of Freetown have passed away, I am convinced that their ideas do live on for us to learn from, to enlarge upon, and pass on to the following generations. I am happy to see how many young people are going back to the land and to the South. They are interested in natural farming and they seem to want to know how we did things in the past, to learn firsthand from those who worked hard, loved the land, and relished the fruits of their labor. I hope that this book will be helpful to them. But above all, I want to share with everyone who may read this a time and a place that is so very dear to my heart.

Spring

Each season had a particular interesting feature, but spring held something special. After the long spell of winter we welcomed the first warm day of February, heralding the coming of spring.

Often a mother hen would surprise us with a healthy brood of baby chickens that she had hatched in the hayloft and somehow gotten down to the ground. They would be chirping and pecking in the snowy slush of the barnyard. We would pick them up and carry them and the mother into the kitchen and place them in a wooden box behind the cookstove which served as a nursery for early hatched chickens, baby calves, pigs, and lambs that were too weak and un-aggressive to compete for food. All such animals would be kept in the kitchen until the severe cold weather was over and they were strong enough to feed themselves. The quiet routine of the kitchen would give way to the sounds of chirping, pip pip, and baa baa. We were so excited about our kitchen guests that we would set about adopting the most unusual ones for ourselves and we would keep watch over our pick sometimes for a year, or until it was sold, which would be a sad day for us. But there was always a good reason given why it had to be sold. All the realities of life were explained to us as we grew up.

Further evidence of spring would be the arrival of the noisy kill-deer, running over the ground as if it were on roller skates, signaling that it was time to begin ploughing. It continued to call out "kill dee, kill dee," during the ploughing season.

I will never forget spring mornings in Virginia. A warm morning and a red sun rising behind a thick fog gave the image of a pale pink veil supported by a gentle breeze that blew our thin marquisette curtains out into the room, leaving them to fall lazily back. Being awakened by this irresistible atmosphere we would hop out of bed, clothes in hand, rush downstairs, dress in a sunny spot, and rush out to the barn to find a sweet-faced calf, baby pigs, or perhaps a colt. We always stopped by the hen house to look at the setting hens sitting in their row of nests along the wall. They had to be checked often to see if the eggs were moist enough to hatch properly. I can still remember the moist smell of chickens hatching and making quiet, cuddly noises. The mother hen would fuss and ruffle her feathers, very annoyed at my mother for lifting her from the nest to sprinkle the eggs. There would be guineas setting under the woodpile where no one could reach and they would appear one day with a brood that was so swift of movement that one could only get a glimpse of them scampering through the weeds.

This was truly a time of birth and rebirth in barnyard, field, and forest. Early morning visits to the barnyard extended into the woods as well, which was just across the stream from the barn. The quiet beauty in rebirth there was so enchanting it caused us to stand still in silence and absorb all we heard and saw. The palest liverwort, the elegant pink lady's-slipper displayed against the velvety green path of moss leading endlessly through the woods. Birds flitting back and forth knowing it was spring and looking for food, a spider winding in his catch while his beautiful dew-laden web shimmered and glistened in the early morning sunshine, the early morning sound of the mournful dove, the caw caw of a crow looking for food.

A stream, filled from the melted snows of winter, would flow quietly by us, gurgling softly and gently pulling the leaf of a fern that hung lazily from the side of its bank. After moments of complete exhilaration we would return joyfully to the house for breakfast. Floating out to greet us was the aroma of coffee cooking and meat frying, mingled with the smell of oak wood burning in the cookstove. We would wash our hands and take our places on the bench behind the table made for the children.

Breakfast was about the best part of the day. There was an almost mysterious feeling about passing through the night and awakening to a new day. Everyone greeted each other in the morning with gladness and a real sense of gratefulness to see the new day. If it was a particularly beautiful morning it was expressed in the grace. Spring would bring our first and just about only fish—shad. It would always be served for breakfast, soaked in salt water for an hour or so, rolled in seasoned cornmeal, and fried carefully in home-rendered lard with a slice of smoked shoulder for added flavor. There were crispy fried white potatoes, fried onions, batter bread, any food left over from supper, blackberry jelly, delicious hot coffee, and cocoa for the children. And perhaps if a neighbor dropped in, dandelion wine was added. With the morning feeding of the animals out of the way, breakfast was enjoyable and leisurely.

Another pleasure was following the plough. I loved walking barefoot behind my father in the newly ploughed furrow, carefully putting one foot down before the other and pressing it into the warm, ploughed earth, so comforting to the soles of my feet. As I listened to my father sing one of his favorite songs, the chickens from the hen house would flock behind me, picking up all kinds of worms and bugs that were turned up by the plough. The noisy killdeer was still around, guarding her tiny speckled eggs in a nest she had made of small stones. Now and then the plough would turn up roots of a sassafras bush which we would carry into the house and make into a tea for breakfast the next morning. We also enjoyed tea made from a bush that grew along the streams; used only while in the bud stage, it was known as sweet bud.

Planting season was always accompanied by the twilight arrival of the whippoorwill repeating breathlessly and rapidly "whippoorwill! whippoorwill!" Because of the longer hours of daylight, field work could extend into the evening, and dinner was served at midday. First spring meals would always be made of many uncultivated plants. We would relish a dish of mixed greens—poke leaves before they unfurled, lamb's-quarters, and wild mustard. We also had salad for a short period made of either Black-Seeded Simpson, or Grand Rapids, loose-leaf lettuce which bolted as soon as the weather became warm. It was served with thin slices of onion before they begin to shape into a bulb—the tops used as well—in a dressing of vinegar, sugar, and black pepper. It was really more of a soup salad. We would fill our plates after finishing our meal and we adored the sweet and pungent flavor against the crispy fresh flavor of the lettuce and onions.

One usually thinks of lamb as a spring dish but no one had the heart to kill a lamb. The lambs were sold at the proper time and the sheep would be culled—some sold and a few butchered. My mother would usually buy the head and the forequarter of the mutton, which she cooked by braising or boiling and served with the first asparagus that appeared along the fence row, grown from seed the birds dropped. There were the unforgettable English peas, first-of-the-season garden crop cooked and served in heavy cream along with sautéed first-of-the-season chicken. As the new calves came, we would have an abundance of milk and butter, as well as buttermilk, rich with flecks of butter. Rich milk was used in the making of gravies, blanc mange, custards, creamed minced ham, buttermilk biscuits, and batter breads, as well as sour-milk pancakes. And we would gather wild honey from the hollow of oak trees to go with the hot biscuits and pick wild strawberries to go with the heavy cream.

Freetown was a beehive of activity, with everyone caring for crops of new animals, poultry, and garden, gathering dandelions and setting them to wine. People also helped each other by trading seed, setting hens, and exchanging ideas as well. Although this was a hectic time and visiting was put off for a calmer time of year, the neighbors still found time for unforgettable pleasantries. I remember when I was very little, our neighbor Mrs. Towles came over one bright afternoon and invited me for tea as she often did. As I walked along the path behind her, we came upon a nest of colored candy Easter eggs. I had never seen anything so beautiful in all my five years of life. I asked her how did she think they had gotten there, and she replied casually, "I guess the Easter Rabbit must have left them there for you."

As the weather warmed up and we moved toward summer, the main crops were planted—corn, beans, melons, and peanuts. Sweet potato plants were ready for pulling from the hotbed—a structure made of 4 x 3 x 3 boards stationed in a corner of the garden. The bed was made by filling in a 6-inch layer of fresh stable horse manure that was then covered over with a 4-inch layer of dry oak leaves and a few twigs of green pine needles. A 4-inch layer of old hay was added and that was topped with a 5-inch layer of clean, dry sand. The bed was then covered with a piece of old blanket or canvas and left to heat up for a few days. When the temperature in the hotbed reached 70°, specially selected sweet potatoes were inserted into the sand and the cover replaced. The bed was aired daily, every afternoon when the temperature was at its highest, and sprinkled lightly with warm water during incubation. When the plants reached a height of 5 inches, the bed was left uncovered so that the plants could toughen before setting them in the open ground. Very often other vegetable seed was sown in the bed alongside the potatoes—those were the days before hybrid seed. We would always save our own seed and plant it from year to year. A few of the vegetables we planted are seldom seen today, such as cymlings, almost flat, rounded, white squash with scalloped edges which matured early and was usually served fried; butter beans; a leafy green known as rape; black-eyed peas served puréed; parsnips, salsify, and root celery. The common herbs were sage, purple basil, chervil, horseradish root, and wild thyme. No homestead was complete without an orchard and a grape arbor bearing fragrant sweet dessert grapes. Some of the fruits we loved best and thought the most flavorsome for preserving and keeping were Stayman Winesap apples; Kieffer pears, which were sweet and juicy; a variety of deliciously sweet cherries—blackheart, sour red, and a bluish-pink one called Royal Ann; fragrant round, red plums, as well as damsons; and that famous old fruit, the quince. Almost all these fruits we served stewed or used as a filling for cake, as well as preserving. The garden also included a gooseberry bush. Flowers, too, were an integral part of every homestead, especially perennials such as cowslips, Virginia bluebells, sweet myrrh, rambling roses, and our favorite geranium (which, incidentally, had its origin in Africa, as did the guinea hen, wheat, and many other good things that are part of our table today).

Planting season in Freetown was particularly hectic because everyone planted their crops, set their chickens, and everything else according to the sign of the zodiac. These signs appeared only once in each month and lasted for two or three days. So the ground had to be ready to plant then; if you missed the proper sign, the crop would be thrown back for a month. It was said that seed that blossomed should be planted when the moon was light, whereas vegetables grown underground should be planted in the dark of the moon. Some of these practices still go on today. There used to be a big sigh of relief when planting was over, but then we would plunge right into the work of cultivation and raising the new crop of hatched chickens, turkeys, and barnyard animals, at the same time as we watched the hay ripen and looked toward hay-cutting time.

I remember in spring how the bobwhite used to walk around as a decoy, calling "bobwhite, bobwhite" to his mate as she sat nearby on her first hatch. We felt happy to hear him calling out, thinking that somehow this made everything complete, and we would answer him back, saying, "Bobwhite, bobwhite! Are your peaches ripe?"

AN EARLY SPRING DINNER

Braised Forequarter of Mutton

Thin-Sliced Skillet-Fried White Potatoes

Skillet Wild Asparagus

Salad of Tender Beet Tops, Lamb's-Quarters, and Purslane
Garnished with Chopped Chervil

Yeast Rolls

Butter

Blanc Mange Garnished with Raspberries

Special Butter Cookies

Coffee

After the shearing of the sheep and the culling of the flock, mutton became available for a short period and it was a treat to sit down again to a meal of braised or boiled mutton with thin-sliced fried white potatoes, wild asparagus found along the fence row, and a beautiful dessert made from the abundant supply of milk and garnished with early ripened raspberries.

Braised Forequarter of Mutton

10 to 12 pounds forequarter of mutton   *Serves 5*
¼ teaspoon thyme leaves, fresh or dry
2 teaspoons fresh-ground black pepper

1 tablespoon plus 1 teaspoon soft butter
½ cup chopped onions
½ cup peeled, seeded, and chopped fresh tomatoes
1 small clove garlic (optional)

Have the butcher remove the neck and the bones in the middle and upper part of the meat, and carve the meat out of the ribs. Keep the bones. Wipe the meat over with a damp cloth, and cut away any loose pieces or stamp dye. Sprinkle the meat with the thyme and pepper and place it upon the rack of ribs it was carved from. Tie the meat and ribs together securely with a clean white string. Paint over the top with 1 tablespoon soft butter. The flavor of mutton is so exotic that any seasoning besides salt and pepper and a little thyme will ruin its special flavor. Place the bones and the meat into a cooking pot. Pound the onion and tomato into a pulp using a mortar or blender, adding 2 cups cold water. Pour the mixture around the meat, cover, and set in a preheated 400° oven. Close the door and turn the oven down to 350°. Cook for 1½ hours before opening again. Check the cooking; the meat should simmer slowly. As it heats through the temperature can be regulated accordingly. Cook for about 3 hours, basting every 20 minutes after the first 1½ hours. If the sauce seems too short, add another cup of hot water. Twenty minutes before the meat is finished sprinkle with a tiny crushed clove of garlic, if you like the flavor of garlic. Remove from the oven, cut away the string, and place the meat on a platter. Set in a warm place. Strain the sauce left in the pan through a fine sieve, skim all the fat from it, and then set on a low burner to heat (but not boil) while the meat is being sliced. Put a teaspoon of soft butter into the sauce, stir vigorously, and pour over the sliced mutton.

Note: The leg of mutton can be treated in the same manner. If fresh tomatoes were not available, canned ones that had been put up during canning season were used.

For recipe for **Thin-Sliced Skillet-Fried White Potatoes,**
see page 208

Skillet Wild Asparagus

1 large bunch (1½ to 2 pounds) asparagus　　*Serves 5*
2 tablespoons butter
Salt and pepper

Skillet-cooked asparagus have more flavor than steamed asparagus. They finish off bright green in color, brittle, and have a flavor of the butter they cooked in. They may be fried whole or cut into 2-inch pieces. If cooked in pieces, the tips should not be added until the stalks are nearly done, as the tips cook more quickly and have a tendency to scorch. If cooked whole, they must be watched carefully.

Rinse the asparagus in cold water. Place the butter in a medium skillet, then put the asparagus on top; the bit of water left clinging is enough. Cover the skillet and let cook about 3 minutes. Be sure they don't burn; remove the lid and check, turning them over. Cover again and let cook for about 5 minutes more. Season to taste after cooking.

Salad of Tender Beet Tops, Lamb's-Quarters, and Purslane
Garnished with Chopped Chervil

We often served an early spring salad of garden beet tops and other green leaves growing wild in the garden, tossed with tender garden lettuce. This called for a different kind of dressing which could be mixed at the table from our canister.

DRESSING

¼ cup cider vinegar
1 teaspoon salt
¼ teaspoon dry mustard
½ teaspoon fresh-ground black pepper
½ cup olive oil

Spring greens (beet tops, lamb's-quarters,
    purslane, young lettuce)
1 tablespoon chopped chervil

It is easier to use a bottle or a small glass jar for mixing salad dressing. Shake vinegar and salt together until dissolved, then add the
mustard and pepper. Shake well again, then add olive oil and shake
until it becomes thick and grayish. That is the moment to sprinkle
it over the leaves and toss. You can always tell whether your dressing
is well balanced when it becomes thick and grayish; if it doesn't, you
have used too much vinegar, so add some more oil.

   Pour the dressing over the greens and toss. Sprinkle with chopped
chervil.

Yeast Rolls from Sponge Batter

SPONGE   *Makes about 36 rolls*

4 medium-sized potatoes
3 cups cold water
3 tablespoons sugar
1 tablespoon dry active yeast, or 1 small cake
    (about ½ ounce) fresh yeast
6 tablespoons sifted flour

BATTER

7 cups sifted unbleached white flour
1 cup tepid milk
2 medium-sized eggs, beaten
2 teaspoons salt
3 tablespoons lard
2 tablespoons butter

1 ½-gallon glass jar
1 5-gallon container*
2 8 x 8 x 2-inch baking pans
1 small bread pan
1 large wooden spoon

Wash and boil potatoes in their skins in the 3 cups water. Boil
briskly until soft—25 to 30 minutes—then remove the potatoes, reserving the water they were cooked in. Peel and mash the potatoes
well while they are still warm. Measure out a cupful of mashed
potatoes in the ½-gallon glass jar and add 1 cup of the tepid potato
water. (If there isn't enough potato water, add enough cold water to
fill a cup.) Add sugar, yeast, and flour to the glass jar. Stir the mixture lightly, then turn down a teacup over the mouth of the jar. Set
overnight in a warm spot to "work." The temperature need not be
as high as 80° for this sponge; it will ferment under slightly cooler
conditions. After setting overnight the sponge will be aromatic and
light as sea foam and ready to mix with the flour.

Place the flour in a large mixing bowl. Pour in the sponge. Stir
with a wooden spoon until well mixed. Pour in the tepid milk and
beaten eggs and salt. Over a pan of hot water, melt half the lard and
1 tablespoon of the butter and mix into the batter. Continue to stir
in a circular motion until the dough becomes rather smooth and

---

* We always used a large container—the preserving kettle, in fact—so we
could leave the dough overnight and it wouldn't run over. If you are going to
be around to watch the dough, use two smaller containers instead.

comes off in a sheet when lifted up on a spoon. This takes about 15 minutes of stirring. Spoon the dough into a deep, well-greased 5-gallon container or two smaller ones. Set in an 80° draft-free place. Cover lightly with a clean cloth. In summer temperatures it is no problem and is a real joy to make yeast breads.

The dough can be set to rise from 4 to 5 hours. Push it down twice during the period of rising, greasing hands with shortening mixture, and gently pushing down the dough, which should be light and bubbly. When the dough has doubled for the second time have at hand the baking pans and the remaining lard and butter melted together. Pinch off a piece of dough the size of a golf ball. Dip fingertips into the melted shortening and grease the dough, rolling it over to make a ball shape. Place each roll in the baking pan close enough to touch the other rolls. Repeat the operation until pans are filled. Each pan takes in 18 rolls. Form remaining dough into a loaf and place in greased bread pan. Set in a warm place to rise ½ inch or a bit more above the pan. Bake in a preheated 425° oven 40 minutes. Remove from the oven, and let set in the pans for about 5 minutes. Remove from the pans and serve hot.

Print of Butter

The centerpiece of every table in Freetown was a pressed glass or cut-glass butter dish holding a rounded mound of butter indented on the top with a free-form shape made from the end of the butter paddle. Soft butter was liked for buttering hot breads, except in very hot weather when the butter dish would be set in the spring box or well house.

Butter was a homemade product. We would spend a whole day skimming the cream from the top of a number of milk crocks. The wooden churn had to be scalded and filled with water to swell it in order to close the opening that had developed as the wood dried out. The cream was poured in, and Grandpa usually did the churning, sitting on the front porch in warm weather or before the fireplace hearth in winter. Cream turns to butter faster when it is warm.

Mother would spend hours washing the butter by kneading it with wooden paddles. After she had washed all the milk out, the water was poured off and excess water was pressed out by kneading with the butter paddles. Then, after all the water was removed, the salt was worked in. Then the butter was pressed into a 1-pound wooden butter print with a removable bottom. The decorated prints were dipped into cold water to keep the butter from sticking. When the butter was pressed out of the mold it would be beautifully decorated on the top. We kept most of these butter prints in the well house and used them as needed, but sometimes when we had extra we would sell them to stores in town.

Blanc Mange

Spring and early summer was a time when there was an abundance of green grass that meant surplus milk, cream, and butter. Some of the desserts we made then were junket, bread pudding, custard, and blanc mange. I hadn't thought of blanc mange as being a fancy or unusual name, any more than Lahore or Freetown. It was just a delicious dessert with Jordan almonds and fresh or canned fruit.

1 cup unblanched Jordan almonds   *Serves 5*
1⅓ cups cold water
½ cup milk
½ cup heavy cream
⅔ cup sugar
1 tablespoon unflavored gelatine
¼ cup cold water
1 teaspoon almond extract
1 teaspoon vanilla extract
2 teaspoons rum (optional)

GARNISH
2 cups raspberries (or other fruit)

Drop the almonds into boiling water, remove from the burner, and leave the almonds until the water cools enough to pick them out. Then slip them out of their skins. Pound the blanched almonds to paste in a mortar or grind them in a nut grinder or blender. Then put the pounded or ground almonds into a blender 2 tablespoons at a time with ⅓ cup water and blend until thoroughly puréed, repeat with the rest until the water and ground nuts are used up. Return the full amount to the blender and blend until the mixture is completely smooth. Combine the milk, the cream, and sugar and add, blending a second time. Strain into a saucepan. Dissolve the gelatine in ¼ cup cold water, add it to the saucepan, and set over medium-high burner, stirring all the while. Bring to a scald but don't allow the mixture to boil. Add the almond extract and the vanilla (rum may be used if desired). Strain and pour into a wet ring mold. Leave overnight. When ready to serve, run a spatula close against the mold, turn out on a serving platter, and garnish with raspberries.

Special Butter Cookies

These cookies are perfectly simple. For generations they have been made in our family repeatedly, and they remain the most delicious type of sugar cookie. For good success, they must be made in accordance with the recipe.

4 ounces (1 stick) butter   *Makes 45 to 50 cookies*
¾ cup granulated sugar
2 medium-sized eggs, beaten
2 cups sifted, all-purpose unbleached flour
1 teaspoon Royal Baking Powder
2 level teaspoons sifted fresh-ground ginger
2 tablespoons light cream, or milk
1 cup crushed cube sugar

Cream together the butter and granulated sugar. Add the beaten eggs and mix well. Add in the flour that has been sifted with the baking powder and the ginger. Mix well. Add in the cream or milk. Mix well again. Spoon the dough onto a small platter or Pyrex dish. Cover securely with wax paper and set in the refrigerator overnight. It may be set into your freezer compartment for 30 minutes or until the dough becomes firm to the touch of a spatula. This is a very soft dough and must be chilled to handle. Lightly dust a rolling surface and just spade out enough dough to roll. It is good to have a chilled rolling pin. Cut before the dough softens too much to handle. Roll the dough out evenly to ⅛ of an inch or a fraction better and cut with a cookie cutter. Lift the cookies from the rolling surface with a spatula and place on cookie sheet. After the cookies have been rolled out and removed, don't try rolling the trimmings. It won't work. Instead, put the free-form pieces of trimmings onto a separate cookie sheet. Sprinkle each one with a bit of crushed cube sugar. Set the cookies into a preheated 400° oven for 8 to 10 minutes.

Cooking time really depends upon how brown one likes the cookies to be. Different degrees of browning change the flavor of the cookies. If one likes a delicate flavor, they should be just the palest brown color. Too much browning spoils the good taste of the cookie. Remove the cookies from the pan and place them on a rack to cool. Store in a clean, airtight tin.

Note: A heavy cookie sheet is best or, if you haven't one, place a second sheet under the one holding the cookies. Otherwise, the cookies will brown too much on the bottom. Sometimes it's well to remove the bottom sheet halfway through the cooking so that the bottom of the cookies will become evenly browned with the top.

A SPRING BREAKFAST

Pan-Fried Shad with Roe
Oven-Cooked Bacon
Scrambled Eggs
Steamed Whole Hominy
Corn Pone
Butter
Wild Strawberry Preserves
Honey from Woodland Bees
Coffee
Dandelion Blossom Wine

Because shad was practically the only fish we ever ate and spring was the only time it was ever seen, we were always much too excited to wait for dinner, so we'd cook it for breakfast whenever it was caught. First we would eagerly search the head for pearls, always hoping to find one. I don't know how we came to expect pearls in the head of the shad except that it did have what looked like a pearl, the size of a large grain of corn and the same shape. We always served shad with scrambled eggs, bacon, steamed hominy, new-found honey, soft, rich batter bread, delicious cold milk, hot coffee, and a sip of dandelion wine. It was truly a meal to celebrate the coming of the spring.

Pan-Fried Shad with Roe

In city fish markets you will very often find shad filleted, split, and boned, but you can also buy a whole shad, which is the way we used to have it. But be sure it is a roe shad. The buck shad is of a brighter color and has more bones throughout the flesh. Shad can be served fried or baked. We preferred it fried. Frying gave a crusty outside while the inside remained tender and juicy. The roe was cooked and served along with it. Shad is one of the very few things left to enjoy that still come but once a year—spring being the only time it leaves the ocean and comes into the fresh waters along the Virginia coast to spawn. April and May is the time.

A 5- to 6-pound shad with roe   *Serves 5 to 6*
4 teaspoons salt
2 cups fine-ground cornmeal
1 teaspoon fresh-ground black pepper
2 slices smoked pork shoulder or bacon
1 cup lard
⅓ cup cold water
4 tablespoons butter
⅓ lemon
2 teaspoons finely cut parsley

Cut the shad into 4-inch pieces and place them in a large mixing bowl. Add the roe, being careful not to break the skin. Sprinkle 2½ teaspoons salt over the fish and roe and cover with cold water, letting stand for 30 to 40 minutes. It will enhance the flavor of the shad. Remove the roe and shad from the salt water, drain. Mix the cornmeal, pepper, and 1½ teaspoons salt together and coat the pieces of fish on both sides and ends. Place the coated pieces on a sheet of wax paper and leave to rest for 30 minutes to an hour to give the meal time to adhere to the fish. Heat a large skillet and toss in slices of pork. When fat is well rendered, remove pork slices and add ½ cup of the lard. Heat until the pan of fat becomes sizzling hot but not smoking. Place in the pieces of fish and see that the fat comes up to about two thirds of the fish. Cook to a golden brown, about 7 minutes on each side. Meanwhile, set the roe to cook in a small skillet with ⅓ cup cold water. Cover loosely and cook gently until all water evaporates, then add butter and sauté for a few minutes. Squeeze over the lemon and sprinkle with parsley. Serve roe along with fried shad. See to it that the roe does not become too dried out.

Oven-Cooked Bacon or Ham

"Oven-cooked bacon" covered many cuts of pork, such as jowl, shoulder, middling, and ham, always cured and sliced ¼ inch thick or a bit less. The rind was usually left on. The meat was rinsed in lukewarm water to remove some of the salt, then placed in a warm skillet and set over the hot section of the stove. When the pan became fully heated and the meat began to fry, it was transferred to the floor of the hot oven or the lower shelf so as not to interfere with other food cooking. A great advantage of oven cooking is that the meat never curls, no matter how thin. It can be cooked without worry about burning but must be checked on sometimes and needs turning over. When well cooked and browned it is delicious. The rind becomes crisp and crunchy and the bacon has a rich, baked flavor.

All types of bacon can be cooked this way—it takes about 15 minutes.

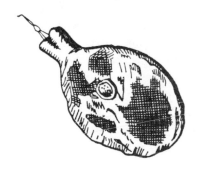

Scrambled Eggs

9 eggs   *Serves 5 to 6*
4 tablespoons cold water
2 teaspoons butter

We used to break the eggs into a jar, add the water, cover it, and shake well. If you have a blender, it does the job, but turn it on for only half a second. Then pour the eggs into a warm, lightly greased skillet. Cook over a medium-low flame, pushing the eggs aside with a spoon as they solidify until all is solid but still moist. Remove immediately from the pan while still soft. Eggs have a tendency to dry out very quickly. Serve right away on a warm platter. Garnish with bacon.

Steamed Whole Hominy

Corn was the backbone of the diet in Freetown for both the people and their stock. Of the variety of ways it was used, transforming dried corn into hominy seemed a most miraculous process. My Aunt Jennie Hailstalk was expert at the making of hominy. One morning when I was visiting her, noticing again the big iron pot on the back of her cookstove, I asked her to explain to me how she did it.

First, she told me, hardwood ashes (about 2 gallons) were boiled for 10 minutes in 4 gallons of cold water. The water was then drained away and put aside, the ashes were discarded, and the water was returned to the pot. Three quarts of shelled, whole-grain white corn were put into the solution over a medium-high fire and cooked for 25 to 30 minutes, then left to steep for an hour after the cooking had stopped.

The corn was then removed from the lye solution and put into a large pan of clean water. At that point she would rub the grains together in her hands and the hull or the husk would slip off. The grains would be rinsed a number of times until the water became clear and all the specks were removed.

Now she set the grains to cook gently until tender (about an hour), stirring constantly and skimming to keep them from burning on the bottom. By this time they would have swelled, doubled in size, and be glistening white. The hominy was put in a colander and set to steam over simmering water until ready to serve, about 10 to 15 minutes.

The hominy had a delicious flavor. It was always served at breakfast and the gravy or natural sauce from cooked meats would be spooned over it. With or without sauce, it was very tasty. Hominy is still being made that way in homes in the South, but you can buy it fully cooked or canned not only in stores in Orange, Virginia, but also in many city supermarkets that stock it or will get it for you.

Note: The cooked solution of hardwood ashes and water is called lye solution; we made soap with it as well. The hardwood we used was oak. The corn was fresh-shelled from the barn.

Corn Pone

Corn pone was a delicious equivalent of the ash cake and is legendary in our history. A beautiful poem was written by one of our early great poets, Paul Laurence Dunbar, entitled "When Mammy Says de Blessing and de Cone Pone's Hot." When there was need for a quick hot snack, we would light the cookstove and stir up some cornmeal and make a number of corn pones, sometimes adding cracklings to make them more interesting, but they were just as delicious plain. The rather stiff batter would be shaped with both hands, fingers closed, to make a large egg shape—the shape of your hand. The pones were about 3 inches wide, and were placed an inch apart on a baking sheet. Baked in a fairly hot oven, when done they were golden brown in color and very crusty outside, which made them more delicious. We would cut them in half and butter them.

2 cups water-ground white cornmeal
1 teaspoon Royal Baking Powder
½ teaspoon salt
⅔ cup cold water
½ cup milk
1 tablespoon melted lard or butter

Makes 4 pones,
about 3 inches wide,
1½ inches high,
and 4 inches long

Sift the meal, baking powder, and salt into a mixing bowl. Add the water and milk. Stir well, add melted fat, and let the mixture rest for 10 minutes. Then take the batter and shape it into pones by cupping both hands together and patting it into form. Place each pone upon a baking sheet an inch apart from the others and bake in a pre-heated 375° oven for 15 to 20 minutes—no longer or the bread will dry out.

Wild Strawberry Preserves

1 pound wild strawberries
1 pound sugar

Makes 4 5-ounce jars

1 2-quart mixing bowl
1 wooden or silver spoon
1 nonmetallic pan (Pyrex, Corning Ware, or
  enamel-covered iron)
4 5-ounce sterilized jars and lids
Paraffin

Wash the berries and place them on a clean, dry cloth to drain. When well drained, remove the caps and put the berries into a mixing bowl. Sprinkle sugar over them and mix gently with a wooden or silver spoon. Cover with a cloth and place in a cold place overnight. Next morning, spoon the berry mixture into a nonmetallic pan and set over a medium-high burner. Bring to a brisk boil, and then cook for only 5 minutes, skimming off any scum on the surface. (Boiling seems to keep the scum in one spot; when not boiling the scum spreads over the surface of the preserves and disappears.) After 5 minutes, remove from the burner, let cool a bit, and with a slotted spoon spoon out the berries into a bowl. Boil the syrup again for 4 minutes only, then pour over the berries. Leave the berries in the syrup to plump until evening. Pour the preserves into the sterilized jars to within ⅛ inch of the top. Fill the rest with paraffin. When the paraffin cools, screw on the covers and store in a dry, cool place.

Note: Brief boiling will help to keep the strawberries from losing their clear bright-red color. Overcooking will cause the syrup to become brown.

Honey from Woodland Bees

Honey was another one of nature's contributions to spring. On warm spring mornings my father would bring in a big pan of honey that he had located in the hollow of an oak tree. He would break into the comb and gather the honey, filling his pan with the delicious, clear, dark amber nectar. We chewed on the wax for days and enjoyed the honey on hot biscuits throughout spring.

The time calculated for gathering was told in a rhyme:

> A swarm of bees in May is worth a load of hay.
> A swarm of bees in June is worth a silver spoon.
> A swarm of bees in July is not worth a fly.

By July the larvae had begun to hatch and spoiled the honey.

Coffee
or Java (as we called it)

The smell of coffee cooking was a reason for growing up, because children were never allowed to have it and nothing haunted the nostrils all the way out to the barn as did the aroma of boiling coffee. The decision about coffee was clear and definite and a cook's ability to make good coffee was one of her highest accomplishments. Mother made real good coffee but some mornings my father would saddle the horse and ride more than a mile up the road to have his second cup with his cousin Sally, who made the best coffee ever.

Morning was incomplete without that cup of well-boiled coffee with cream from overnight milk, which was stirred in to make a mocha-colored kind of coffee syllabub. The froth on the coffee was quickly chased around the cup with a spoon and spooned into the mouth before it vanished. It was said that this froth signified unexpected money coming to the one who drank the coffee. Coffee went well with hot breads, butter, and meats with gravies.

Coffee also separated people by age. As I said, we children weren't allowed to drink it and aged aunts, uncles, and grandparents never drank coffee from a cup. That was a waste of time. Every aged person in Freetown drank their coffee from a bowl.

All cooks arrived at making good coffee from different methods. Some added salt, some eggshells, others whites or only yolks, and all were divine. On any sunny morning you would see everyone's coffee pot hanging out on the garden fence post airing out after the morning's coffee.

Coffee came in a container, just as the present-day cereal packages do. It was wax-lined and the grains never seemed to have lost their strength. Long boiling didn't seem to make the coffee bitter, either. Of course, everyone used high-quality enamel pots and well water. And coffee trees hadn't yet been tampered with by the experimental stations.

Good coffee can be made without complicated pots and gadgets and with less coffee than is usually required. Of course, a clean pot, free from highly perfumed soap powders, is important, as is a good brand of coffee that is pretty stable in the market, such as Yuban, Brown Gold, and Martinson's in the blue can for drip. All can be boiled.

Try a coffee-house blend of ½ pound Colombia, ½ pound Java, and ¼ pound French roast. Also, green coffee beans can be roasted and ground at home with good success but it takes great patience. The beans are usually browned on top of the stove using an iron frying pan, and stirring all the while, but they can be roasted successfully in the oven—at 400° for 18 minutes, shaking the pan once during the roasting. When a bean is crushed it should be of a dark chocolate-brown color through and through. Once browned it is very simple to put beans into a hand coffee mill and grind fine. When making coffee with the boiled method, use only a small amount until the right strength is achieved.

It is of little value to grind beans unless they have been just roasted or at least heated up again in the oven. It is the fresh roasting that matters. A two or three days' supply can be roasted and ground with good results.

If one must have another way of brewing coffee a drip pot can be successful if you use a 6-cup pot for only up to 4 cups of water. Use 2 level tablespoons of coffee for each 6 ounces of water. Boil 4 cups of water, and when it is near boiling pour in about ¼ cup of water over the grounds and turn the burner up under the rest of the water. Bring to a furious boil and pour onto the moistened grounds all at once. Cover, and the minute the dripping is just about finished, remove the grounds right away. The problem with drip coffee is one of serving it piping hot; it changes the flavor to reheat it but it can be kept hot with success by holding it in a good silver or heavy metal pot until served. In case you have a wood stove it can rest on the back of that very well until served. But I have found much more success using the recipe on the following page.

Makes 4 cups

> 5 6-ounce cups of cold well water or bottled
>   water
> 5 level tablespoons coffee
> A few grains of salt

Place the coffee, water, and salt in the bottom of a glass Pyrex pot or enameled saucepan. Bring to a quick boil and then turn the burner down. When a boil is reached let simmer for 12 to 13 minutes, or longer if a stronger brew is desired. Spill in a spot of ice-cold water and remove from the burner. Let rest a minute then pour the coffee into a hot pot and serve while piping hot.

Dandelion Blossom Wine

Very early in spring when new green grass blanketed the countryside, suddenly it would be dotted over with the golden blossoms of the dandelion plant. The neighbors would be seen out early in the morning before breakfast picking the golden blossoms. For wine-making, the blossoms must be picked before noon. At midday they close up tight. We were delighted to join in the picking and waited eagerly to watch the blossoms close at midday. Because of the early emergence of the dandelion blossoms they were considered a good tonic when made into wine. It was taken at breakfast and served to visiting friends in brandy glasses. We called it wine but it was more like a liqueur and tasted a bit like clear Drambuie. Everyone around made dandelion wine and exchanged wine, as well as views on it. Some added a piece of orange rind but most used only the blossoms. Oranges were not that available in spring.

Makes about 3 quarts

1 gallon open dandelion blossoms
5 quarts boiling, noncarbonated spring or well
     water
½ unpeeled, seeded orange (optional)
3½ pounds sugar

1 5-gallon stone crock or glass jar
3 1-quart sterilized bottles with corks plus 1 pint
     bottle

Pick the dandelion blossoms far away from polluted areas, in clear, open fields; there will be less bugs and ants.

To prepare for wine, have at hand a good, clean stone crock or Pyrex container, because you will be pouring boiling water over the blossoms and a glass jar will crack and spoil your blossoms. Pick over the blossoms. See to it that there are no spiders or bugs in them. Drop the blossoms into the crock and pour the boiling water over. If using the orange, add it. Cover with a clean white napkin and let stand for 3 days in the kitchen out of the way where it's not too cold. Dandelions come in early spring and for good fermentation warmth is needed. Strain through a thin, clean, odor-free cloth into a clean glass jar. Add the sugar and stir until the sugar dissolves. Cover again with a clean cloth and leave in the kitchen in a warm, draft-free place for 3 weeks. Then strain into clean, dry jars, filling up to the top. Tie a clean cloth over the mouth of each jar and leave in the same place to finish fermenting, which will take about 4 months, or until the wine stops being effervescent. Then strain carefully into clean bottles, leaving behind any sediment that usually settles on the bottom. Fill the bottles nearly full and cork tightly, taking care that the cork is clean and new. Store in a dry, dark place until needed.

Note: Some people add one-half teaspoon of unadulterated yeast to the wine after the blossoms have been strained to raise the alcoholic content but I think it gives a very yeasty taste to the wine.

 # A LATE SPRING LUNCH

Ring Mold of Chicken with Rich Wild-Mushroom Sauce

Slices of Baked Virginia Ham

Crispy Biscuits

Butter

Garden Strawberry Preserves

Salad of Grand Rapids Lettuce Leaves and Romaine
with a Vinegar, Sugar, Salt and Pepper Dressing

Caramel Pie

Coffee

Creamed chicken was an elegant dish for an occasion like Sunday lunch. It was served with a sauce of real cream and wild mushrooms, and not to be skimpy, slices of baked ham went with it. There were always hot biscuits, a spring salad, butter, and for dessert, often a favorite caramel pie.

Ring Mold of Chicken with Rich Wild-Mushroom Sauce

My favorite chicken dish was the ring mold with wild-mushroom sauce served on a beautiful Sunday afternoon in late spring when the doors could be left open and the warm rays of the sun streaked across the dining table, saluting my mother for her efforts in presenting a beautiful meal gathered from field, forest, garden, and barnyard. One never knew what to expect when she returned from the morning feeding and gathering; sometimes it was finding just enough wild mushrooms to flavor a cream sauce worthy of the chicken it was to be spooned over, served with tender green garden lettuce, green beans, and crusty yeast bread.

2 2¾- to 3-pound chickens   *Serves 5 to 6*
2 stalks celery with leaves
7 or 8 peppercorns
3 cups water
1 teaspoon salt
¼ teaspoon black pepper
½ cup skimmed reserved broth
3 beaten egg yolks
¼ cup fine, white bread crumbs
3 egg whites
1 bunch watercress

1 10-inch ring mold

The chicken for a ring mold should be one of good flavor. A Perdue fowl or roasting chicken or one from a good organic food shop is the best I have found. Cook the birds whole. This will help to preserve the flavor. Place them in a pot with the celery, leaves included, and the peppercorns. Add in 3 cups of water. Cover and set on a medium-high burner to start cooking. When simmering begins, turn the burner very low and simmer for 2 hours without allowing the pot to boil. I find that the broth has a much better taste if prevented from boiling. When the chicken is well cooked and tender, drain away the broth and set aside to cool. Skim the fat off and reserve. Cool the chicken a bit, remove the skin, and cut into fine pieces by hand while still warm. There should be enough to fill a quart measure. It is better to do the chopping by hand instead of using a food chopper. The meat will further crumble by mixing. Place the diced

meat into a mixing bowl. Sprinkle in salt, pepper, ½ cup of reserved broth, 3 tablespoons of fat skimmed from the broth, and the
beaten egg yolks. Mix well, and then sprinkle in the bread crumbs,
made from rubbing fresh slices of white bread against a grater.
Beat the egg whites until stiff but not dry, then fold them into the
chicken. Spoon the mixture into a well-buttered 10-inch ring mold.
Place the mold in a pan of hot water and set to cook in a preheated 350° oven for 45 minutes. When finished, remove from the
oven and allow to rest for 10 minutes before unmolding. Turn out
onto a hot platter, fill the center with sprigs of watercress, and garnish the platter with same.

Wild Mushrooms for Picking

Wild mushrooms, especially morels, have a superior flavor to that of
the hothouse variety. They are most delicious and are an elegant accompaniment to any sauce.

First and foremost, pick only what you are sure of—sure-sure-
sure—and only pick young, fresh mushrooms. After all, you
wouldn't buy old mushrooms in the store. Don't wash wild mushrooms; it's ruinous. They'll become mushy and soggy. Just brush the
dirt off.

There is a group called the "Foolproof 4," which cannot be mis-
taken for any other. They are easy to identify, but one must still
study them. They are as follows:

I.   MORELS
      a. pitted tops, almost spongelike;
      b. can be dried.

To most people morels are the most delicious tasting. They appear
in spring—April and May—when the weather is warm and dry.
They grow on the edge of oak forests, in shady, cool pastures, and
in apple orchards.

II. PUFFBALLS
    a. must be *snow white* inside;
    b. can be eaten raw in salads.

They appear in summer and fall in sparse woodlands, pastures, along the footpath, and in orchards.

III. CHICKEN MUSHROOMS
    a. known by this name because of their chicken-like flavor;
    b. orange in color;
    c. grow in clusters on trunks of hardwood trees, from middle of spring to middle of autumn.

IV. SHAGGY MANES
    a. pick when young; turn dark with age and will then produce an inky substance when broken;
    b. they appear in summer and autumn in orchards, gardens, and along footpaths.

If it is impossible to go picking wild mushrooms, all isn't lost. Many fine food departments, such as that in Bloomingdale's, carry wild varieties; two I recommend particularly are Forest Morels by Blanchaude and delicious Field Ceps by Brillat. Both are imported from France and, although canned, they are just delicious.

Rich Wild-Mushroom Sauce

1 pint heavy cream
1 cup wild, fresh mushrooms, or a can of
   imported field mushrooms
½ cup chicken broth with the fat skimmed off
Salt and pepper to taste
¼ cup sherry

Pour the cream into a wide frying pan, 10 to 12 inches. Bring to a vigorous boil and let continue until the cream is reduced by one third, which it will quickly do. Add in mushrooms and simmer a few minutes, then stir in the broth from the chicken. Continue to heat, not cook, for 10 minutes more and, just before serving, reheat and season with salt, pepper, and sherry to taste.

Baked Virginia Ham

Boil the ham first, as directed on page 138. After the ham is boiled and cool enough to handle, slice away the skin and fat, leaving on enough fat (about ½ inch) to keep the lean meat from showing. Sprinkle the fat over with fresh-grated white bread crumbs. Place the ham in a baking pan and set it into a preheated 375° oven. Cook until a rich, golden brown. Remove from the oven and let cool well before slicing. A baked ham can be cooked a day or two ahead. A cured ham will keep well for over a week without refrigeration and for months well refrigerated. A sharp, wide-bladed knife is best for obtaining a nice, wide, thin slice.

For boiling a ham you will need a ham boiler or an enamel lobster pot. We often used a lard can, which can still be found in some hardware stores.

Note: Virginia country hams can be ordered from The Orange Food Bank, Box 166, Orange, Virginia 22960.

For recipe for **Crispy Biscuits,** see page 176.

Garden Strawberry Preserves

3 cups crushed berries   *Makes 5 5-ounce jars*
2½ cups sugar

1 *2-quart non-aluminum saucepan*
5 *5-ounce sterilized jars and lids, or 3 ½-pint jars*
Paraffin

Set the jars in a pan of water over a low burner.

Wash berries in a bowl of cold water to make sure they are free of grit and dust. Remove berries by hand and place them on a clean, dry towel to drain. Then remove the caps and crush the berries slightly with a clean, odorless, wooden pestle or a strong coffee mug. Pour into a non-aluminum saucepan and set over a low flame to heat. Meanwhile, heat the sugar either in a double boiler or in a dish in the oven, being careful not to brown it, but making sure it becomes very hot (about 10 minutes in a 350° oven). Now pour the hot sugar over the berries, turning the burner up while stirring the sugar around. The cooking should be as brisk as possible without scorching; it should take about 9 minutes in all. As soon as the preserves begin to boil up, a scum will rise on the surface; skim it off right away with a wooden or silver spoon. It is much better to skim while it's rapidly boiling, because that seems to cause the scum to remain in a mass and it's easy to dip it out without getting too much of the syrup. After 9 minutes of rapid cooking, pour the preserves into the hot jars, filling to about ⅛ inch from the top. Lift the jars out onto a dry surface to cool. When cold, carefully melt paraffin and pour into the filled jars. When paraffin is cool, put on the lids and seal.

Salad of Grand Rapids Lettuce Leaves and Romaine

Grand Rapids lettuce was a loose-leaf green that was very easy to grow but went to seed quickly in hot weather. Our way of producing it was to sow it along the garden fence near the well. It was covered with brush, and we kept the ground well-watered until the tender leaves were large enough to make a bowl of salad. It was enjoyed with our favorite dressing.

DRESSING   *Serves 4 to 5*
¼ cup vinegar
2 teaspoons sugar
¼ teaspoon salt
⅛ teaspoon fresh-ground black pepper
1 quart lettuce leaves and romaine, broken up
4 or 5 scallions, sliced thin with some green top
    added

Put the vinegar, sugar, salt, and pepper into a bowl or bottle. Shake or stir with a wooden spoon until all the salt has dissolved. Pour it over the lettuce and sliced scallions. Set aside until the rest of the meal is ready to serve. This salad holds for an hour without wilting, as it has no oil. It has an interesting taste given by fresh, tender lettuce, scallions, and vinegar.

Caramel Pie

Brown-sugar caramel pie is another local dessert, known and loved for at least a hundred and fifty years. The ladies of Freetown prided themselves on making the most perfect desserts. One neighbor was very proud of her talent; whenever we visited her she would bring out a pie or tart, and as she served it, she would always say, "Taste it! It'll melt in your mouth!" And it would. This is a very haunting dessert, so rich and sweet one could easily overindulge. It's great after a heavy meal, to be served as tiny tarts or in very slender wedges.

Pastry dough, see page 217   *Makes 2 8-inch pies*

FILLING

3 cups soft dark-brown sugar (not brownulated)
⅛ teaspoon salt
2 tablespoons sifted flour
2 eggs, separated and beaten
2 tablespoons butter, slightly melted over hot
    water
4 tablespoons dark Karo syrup
2 teaspoons vanilla extract
1 cup milk, at room temperature

2 8-inch pie plates or tart pans

Line pie plates or tart pans with pastry and refrigerate.

In a large mixing bowl mix sugar, salt, and flour. Stir well with a clean wooden spoon and stir well again after each addition. Add the beaten yolks, butter, syrup, vanilla, and milk. When well mixed, beat the egg whites to soft peaks and fold in. Pour the batter into chilled, pastry-lined pans. Set into a preheated 350° oven. Bake until set, about 35 to 40 minutes. Remove from the oven. Serve warm. When cut, the filling should be about the consistency of blackberry jelly, not too firm.

A LATE SPRING DINNER

Skillet Spring Chicken with Watercress

Buttered Jerusalem Artichokes or Salsify

Garden Green Peas in Cream

Biscuits

Butter

Pear Preserves

Rhubarb Pie

Coffee

Sitting down to a meal with the first chicken of the season was always a pleasure. It was also the day we removed our shoes for the season—the weather being sufficiently warm—with a feeling of freedom and an awareness of the fullness of spring, and a delicious meal inside us.

Skillet Spring Chicken with Watercress

There was always great excitement when the first chickens from spring hatching were cooked. The neighbors would announce when they expected to have their first spring chicken meal. We all reared our chickens carefully and fed them by hand, which made them especially tender and tasty. The first ones we had were usually pan-broiled.

> 2 squab chickens, halved (baby chickens   *Serves 4*
>   about 1 pound each)
> 6 ounces (1½ sticks) butter
> 1 bunch fresh watercress
> Salt and pepper
>
> *1 12-inch skillet*

Wipe the chickens with a damp cloth; do not season or flour. Set the skillet to heat on a medium-high flame and add in the butter. When the butter begins to sizzle, place the chickens in the skillet, skin side down. Cook until the skin side is a good, brown color, which should take about 12 minutes. Then turn the chickens over, cover, and cook over a medium flame for about 25 minutes. Remove the chickens from the pan and place on a platter on a bed of watercress. Sprinkle with salt and pepper to taste and serve. Season only when cooked. (A better color is achieved when the chicken is not salted and peppered and floured beforehand—and the butter flavor is more pronounced.)

Buttered Jerusalem Artichokes

There were a number of Old World vegetables that were commonly used in late winter and early spring. The Jerusalem artichoke was one—a perennial plant that grows 7 feet high with yellow blossoms in summer. The tubers look like the fresh root of ginger.

We dug them as soon as the ground began to thaw. They were a welcome change in our diet after a winter of dishes made of preserved and dried ingredients.

2 pounds Jerusalem artichokes   *Serves 4 to 5*
Water to cover
¼ cup (½ stick) butter

Wash the unpeeled artichokes and place in a saucepan of cold water
to cover. Bring to a boil and cook briskly for 18 minutes. Drain, slip
the skins off, and serve with melted butter poured over. Garnish, if
you like, with a bit of parsley.

Salsify

Salsify was another late winter root vegetable as commonly used
as carrots. It was sown early in spring while the soil was cool, otherwise germination was poor. It was left alone to grow and mature
through the following winter. We would dig the salsify in early
spring as soon as the ground thawed out. When cooked, it tasted deliciously like oyster stew. The root is slender like that of a carrot and
is a grayish-white color.

2 bunches (about 1 dozen) salsify   *Serves 4 to 5*
1 cup cream
Salt and pepper to taste
2 teaspoons butter

Salsify is cleaned the same way as carrots, by scraping. Plunge
each root into cold water as it is cleaned or it will turn dark. When
all the roots are cleaned, slice into 1-inch pieces and plunge them
into a saucepan of boiling water. Cook briskly for 40 minutes. When
cooked, drain away the water and keep covered.

Heat the cream to boiling. Add salt and pepper and butter. Pour
into the salsify pan and let the contents heat without cooking, until
ready to be served. Salsify can be served simply buttered without

cream, if desired; in either case, it's nice to add a bit of chopped parsley.

Green Peas in Cream

Green peas, or English peas as they were called, were looked upon with high favor and considered a great delicacy among the people of Freetown. Once the peas began to ripen they lasted only about 2 weeks, so there was great excitement when it was discovered that they were ripe enough to pick. If our peas ripened first, they were shared with the neighbors and vice versa. Peas were very flavorful and tender, maturing in early spring. When milk and cream were plentiful, they were served in lots of butter and sweet cream.

When buying peas, it is better to get them when they first come into the market. They are usually more tender; otherwise tender peas and overripe ones are mixed together, and unless you are allowed to pick out the tender pod or pods containing the small peas, you'll be disappointed at the taste.

4 cups cold water   *Serves 4 to 5*
3 cups shelled tender peas
1 tablespoon sugar
1 scant teaspoon salt
1 cup heavy cream
2 tablespoons butter
½ tablespoon finely cut fresh chervil

In a 2-quart saucepan bring 4 cups of water to a rolling boil, and drop in the peas a few at a time so as not to stop the boiling of the water. When all the peas are in, add the sugar and salt. Continue to boil rapidly, uncovered, until tender (it might take 10 minutes for baby peas fresh from the garden or 25 minutes for those in markets today). Drain away the cooking liquid and hold the peas in a warm spot. Pour the cream into a 9-inch skillet, bring to a boil, and let boil rapidly for 1 or 2 minutes, no more, to reduce. Pour the boiling cream over the peas, add butter, and swish the peas around in the pan. Keep hot but do not cook. Sprinkle the chervil over and serve.

For recipe for **Biscuits,** see page 124.

Pear Preserves

At snack time we loved to use pear preserves as a filling for hot biscuits—or even cold ones. Its meaty texture and spicy clove flavor made it so appealing there was seldom any left over once we'd opened a jar.

3 pounds pears, preferably Kieffer   *Makes about 8 or 9*
2½ pounds sugar   *5-ounce jars*
½ cup water
8 whole cloves (tied in clean cheesecloth)

1 5-quart nonmetallic pot
8 or 9 sterilized 5-ounce jars with covers
Paraffin

Peel, core, and slice each pear into about 8 slices. Place them in a 5-quart wide-bottomed nonmetallic pot. Sprinkle over with the sugar, add water and cloves, and set the pot over a low burner until contents begin to simmer. Then raise the heat and cook the pears gently for an hour. Remove them from the burner and leave to sit overnight. Next morning put the pears back on medium burner and cook gently until the syrup thickens and the pears turn a clear amber color, about 45 minutes of cooking. Have heating 8 to 9 sterilized jars.

Remove cloves and fill the hot jars with hot pear preserves to ¼ inch from the top. Then pour melted paraffin over the tops of the jars to fill them completely, and place lids on top. Store in a cool, dark place.

Rhubarb Pie

PASTRY
1½ cups plus 2 teaspoons sifted flour
1 scant teaspoon salt
¼ cup chilled lard
¼ cup cold water

Makes 1 8 or 9-inch pie
(depending on shallowness of pie plate)

FILLING
⅔ cup sugar
¼ teaspoon fresh-grated nutmeg
2 teaspoons cornstarch
4 cups (about 1½–2 pounds) fresh rhubarb, cut
    into ½-inch pieces

1 8 or 9-inch pie plate

Put 1½ cups sifted flour and the salt into a 2-quart bowl, add the chilled lard, and mix well with a pastry blender or with fingertips. This blend will not be as dry as a butter-mixed pastry. When well blended add all of the water and mix until the water is all absorbed. This will make the dough a bit sticky. Sprinkle over lightly with 2 teaspoons of flour and roll into a ball. Leave to rest in a cool place for about 15 minutes.

Separate the dough into two unequal pieces. Roll out the larger piece and place it into a 9-inch pie pan. Roll out the smaller piece and cut it into ¾-inch strips to form a latticework top crust.

Place the strips upon a sheet of wax paper and place it, along with the pastry-lined pie plate, into the refrigerator until needed.

When ready to prepare the filling, remove pastry from refrigerator. Mix together well the sugar, nutmeg, and cornstarch. Sprinkle 3 tablespoons of the sugar mixture over bottom of pastry. Mix the rest into the rhubarb and fill the crust. Place on strips in lattice fashion. Moisten rim of bottom crust to help lattice strips adhere to rim of bottom pastry. Place the pie into a preheated 450° oven.

This high temperature is important in forming a crispy crust when using very juicy products. If the crust tends to brown too quickly, cut a ring of aluminum foil and place it over the rim of the pie. It is the rim that usually overbrowns. Remove the foil about 10 minutes before the pie is to be removed from the oven. Total cooking time for the pie is 40 minutes.

A HEARTY MIDDAY DINNER

Oven Brisket or Rolled Chuck
Sautéed Parsnips
Salad of Lettuce and Scallions with Vinegar Dressing
Crusty Yeast Bread
Butter
Bread Pudding with Boiled Custard Sauce
Coffee

Returning to the house from the field to a midday dinner of the first beef of the season, sautéed fresh-dug parsnips, crispy salad, and a crusty, warm bread pudding was a great satisfaction after a morning of hard work.

Oven Brisket or Rolled Chuck

Beef was more available in the spring and summer and it was inexpensive as well, being locally butchered. We would take a big piece so that we could have some left for slicing cold during the busy season. Usually it was the rib roast. It was dusted with flour, salt, pepper, cooked to perfection, and served cold after the first or second meal. Locally grown beef had such a great flavor. None was ever left to spoil.

Because of the lack of flavor in beef today, I have searched and found that the more unpopular cuts have a bit more taste. Brisket, rolled chuck, which is also sold sliced as chicken steak, and flanken all have more flavor than some of the other more expensive, better-known cuts.

For preparing this dish of brisket or chuck, purchase half as many onions as beef.

> 3 pounds beef brisket or chuck   *Serves 6*
> Vegetable oil or lard
> 1 tablespoon butter
> 1½ pounds onions, peeled and sliced
> Fresh-ground black pepper
> 3 or 4 whole allspice
> 1 bay leaf
> Salt

Wipe the meat with a damp cloth. Heat a skillet hot, grease lightly with oil or lard, and add the beef, searing well on all sides until well browned. Place the seared meat in a heavy pot or pan. Wipe the skillet out and then add a tablespoon of butter and put in the onions. Stir the onions until they are pretty well browned. Sprinkle the meat over with fresh-ground black pepper and now add the browned onions, allspice, and bay leaf. Cover closely and see that the pan is good and hot before placing it in the oven. Set into a preheated 400° oven until the meat begins to cook. Turn the oven to 225° and leave to cook undisturbed for 2½ hours. When finished, remove the meat and press the onions through a sieve. Add to pan drippings and season this sauce with salt and pepper to taste. Serve hot with the beef.

Sautéed Parsnips

4 medium-sized parsnips   *Serves 5 to 6*
2 tablespoons butter
Salt and pepper

Scrape the parsnips and set them to cook in a saucepan of boiling water. Cook until tender, about 25 minutes. Remove from cooking liquid. When cool, slice in half and sauté in a hot skillet with 2 tablespoons of butter. When golden brown on each side, season with salt and pepper, remove to a platter, and serve hot.

Salad of Lettuce and Scallions

There were no special rules on the serving of salads. Salads were served in accordance with the season of the particular leafy greens —the first being the salad below. Later, there were beet tops, lamb's-quarters, purslane, and Cos lettuce. And in the middle of summer these would be used for salad instead of boiled leafy greens, such as rape, dandelion leaves, wild mustard, and beet top.

A part of every table's centerpiece were the butter dish, as I've mentioned, the spoon holder, and a canister of jars holding vinegar, oil, mustard, sugar, Worcestershire sauce, and pepper. Everyone was free to mix his or her own dressing for the salad.

The first salad of spring consisted of scallions or young onion plants, before they had reached the bulb stage, and Simpson, a tender kind of lettuce that contained three or four leaves and grew to about 3 inches tall. These were the first salad greens gathered. The scallions were sliced very thin and the green tops were used as well. The lettuce has so few leaves that we had to gather a pailful to have enough for the meal. This type of salad was of short duration; as the weather heated up, the onion plants began to develop into bulbs and the lettuce went to seed. But when available we served it every day, from late April through May, until it became too tough to use. The dressing was made of sugar, vinegar, salt, and pepper. No oil was used in the dressing and that kept the greens always crisp and crunchy.

We would eat the salad last, so that we could spoon lots of dressing onto our plates. The sweet and pungent dressing gave a nice flavor to the tasty, crispy lettuce and scallions. Recipe for dressing is on page 34.

Crusty Yeast Bread

Of the variety of breads we used to make, I have tried to pick those that I remembered to be less complicated, although there are no shortcuts in the making of good bread. The most important requirements are warmth, good ingredients, and proper rising of the dough. Yeast without preservatives and water without chemicals helps the bread to rise quickly and will also give it a delicious flavor. No one in Freetown knew about BHT or fluoridated water. The rising of the dough is most important, and proper warmth is essential. If conditions are not normally warm, it is good to put a wide pan of warm, not too hot, water on the stove or table, then to place a wire rack over it and set the bowl of dough on the rack. The wide pan will radiate warmth all around the bowl and hasten rising. Check often to keep the water warm.

This recipe requires no kneading. Proper rising is the key to this dough.

SPONGE   *Makes 4 loaves*
1 cup unbleached white flour
1 tablespoon sugar
1 teaspoon salt
1 package (1 tablespoon) dry active yeast, or 1
    small cake (½ ounce) fresh yeast, dissolved
    in ¼ cup lukewarm water

½ cup milk
½ cup water

FLOUR MIXTURE
1 rounded tablespoon lard
¾ cup hot water
2 cups unbleached white flour
1 cup whole-wheat flour

Place 1 cup flour, the sugar, salt, and dissolved yeast into a large mixing bowl. Mix well. Heat the milk and add to flour mixture together with the water. Stir lightly and set the bowl in a warm (80° to 90°), draft-free place to rise for 25 minutes.

Add the lard to the hot water and set aside to melt and cool until the sponge is ready.

To achieve a crusty texture in this bread, take an 8- to 10-inch iron pan and set it on the floor of the oven when you start preheating the oven. Leave it there until the bread is set into the oven. The minute the bread is placed in, pour a cupful of cold water into the hot iron pan and quickly close the door. The steam developed from pouring the water into the hot pan will help in the rising and the shaping of the bread as well as the crust.

When the yeast sponge is ready (it should be light and bubbly) add to it the flour, stir, and add in the water and lard mixture. Stir well and return to a warm spot to rise twice the size of the original dough. Once the dough has doubled, gently push it down again and let it rise and double once more. Turn the dough onto a floured surface, shape, smooth the dough over, and divide into four equal parts. Take each piece of dough and roll it into a sausagelike shape by lightly rolling the piece of dough away from you. This is done by rolling with both hands open and pushing away as you press until the proper shape and length (about 8 inches) has been obtained. Place three of the loaves side by side about 2 inches apart on a cookie sheet to rise. You'll have to use another smaller sheet for the fourth loaf if you can fit both in your oven—otherwise leave the fourth loaf to roll out while the others are being baked. Place the loaves to rise in the same warm spot. When fully risen, in about 25 to 30 minutes, they will be light to the touch and about double their original size. Make 4 incisions across the top of each loaf about ½ inch deep with a sharp, clean razor blade and set them into a preheated 425° oven. Pour a cup of cold water into the iron pan that is heating on the floor of the oven (see above). After 15 minutes the pan can be removed while the bread continues to cook. Turn the heat to 375° for the rest of the cooking—another 10 minutes. After the bread is cooked a total of 25 minutes, remove from the oven and place it to rest on a wire rack for a few minutes before serving.

Note: The recipe can be made with all white flour if desired. It is just more interesting in texture with a cup of whole-wheat flour.

✓Bread Pudding

Bread pudding and other custard dishes were popular in the early spring because of new calves and new green grass producing extra pails of milk, and a good way to use up some of the stale bread was to make bread pudding. I can still remember entering the kitchen, which was detached from the main house, and there, cooling on a table near the door, would be a big pan of delicious-looking bread pudding, filling the air with the rich smell of butter and nutmeg rising from the layers of bread that were submerged in a custard of rich milk, fresh country eggs, and plump raisins. When served, a bowl of custard would be passed to spoon over if needed. Of course, you can make a pudding using one layer of bread and leaving lots of custard beneath to spoon over. Times have changed and today's bread is not of the same quality of home-baked.

To make a flavorsome pudding, the bread should be buttered liberally on the bottom side. The best bread for this is the preceding crusty yeast bread—or any French or Italian-style bread is good. It also has a good shape, giving the pudding a nice-looking topping when baked. Lots of grated nutmeg is what really makes a bread pudding. Grate it liberally.

8 to 10 1-inch slices of dry French bread   *Serves 5 to 6*
½ cup (1 stick) soft butter
4 medium-sized eggs
⅔ cup granulated sugar
4 cups rich sweet milk
2 teaspoons vanilla extract
⅓ nutmeg, grated
3 tablespoons raisins
3 tablespoons crushed cube sugar

1 10 x 10-inch ovenproof dish, buttered well

Remove crusts from bread and butter one side of bread. Crack eggs into a large mixing bowl, beat well with a fork, add in ⅔ cup sugar and stir well. Pour in the milk, stirring as you pour. Add vanilla and a good grating of the piece of nutmeg. Boil some water and drop the raisins into it. Remove after 10 minutes and let cool in a strainer. Strain the egg-milk mixture into a pitcher for pouring, place the buttered bread in the buttered casserole, sprinkle in the raisins, and grate in some more nutmeg. Pour in the custard mixture and grate over the rest of the nutmeg. The casserole should only be two thirds filled. Sprinkle over all the crushed cube sugar. Place a wire rack in a baking pan. Set the pudding on the wire rack, fill the baking pan with hot water, and set into a preheated 350° oven. Close the door and turn the heat down to 325°. Bake for 40 minutes, seeing to it that the custard never bakes too fast or it will separate. Serve hot with custard sauce.

Boiled Custard Sauce

3 egg yolks, beaten
Pinch of salt
¼ cup sugar
2 cups milk
Bowl of ice water
2 teaspoons vanilla extract

Beat the yolks in a bowl. Add in salt and sugar and stir well with spoon. Heat the milk to the scalding point, which is reached when tiny beads begin to gather around the edges of the milk. Remove from the burner and pour the milk into the bowl with the beaten egg yolks, stirring as you pour. Clean the saucepan and pour in the milk and egg mixture. Place over medium burner, stirring constantly until the custard shows a definite coating of the spoon. When this takes place, remove pan from burner and set it into a bowl of ice water, stirring continuously for a few minutes. Add vanilla and stir again. Pour the custard into a pitcher or bottle. Serve warm.

Summer

The busy season of harvesting and canning brought many delights at mealtime: deep-dish blackberry pie, rolypoly, summer apple dumplings, peach cobblers, and always pound cake to accompany the fruits or berries that would be left from canning. There would also be unexpected meat dishes whenever the hay mower clipped the legs of rabbits and quail that were feeding or living in the hay-field. Whenever these creatures heard the mower coming, they would crouch down, making themselves perfect targets for the mower blade. Once they were damaged they would have to be killed and dressed, then left to age a day or two. Then there would be a surprise dinner of fried or smothered rabbit with the quail added in. If the quail turned out to be a hen, we would hunt for her nest and, when we found the eggs, we'd set them under a bantam or give them to someone who had a hen. After they hatched, the quail chicks would stay with the domestic hen until they were big enough to return to the wild.

Another surprise would be a turtle soup. After a thunderstorm that brought heavy rain, the streams would be washed out and turtles left in the field. We would always run outside after a storm to see what had happened, and often we would discover a turtle making its way to the house. And we knew immediately that that turtle would end up in a pot of soup.

The main crop of garden vegetables would be coming in at this time: new cabbage, potatoes, cymling (a white squash nearly flat and round with scalloped edges), butter beans, string beans, tomatoes, eggplant, and roasting ears. Green corn was always referred to as roasting ears. Actually, we knew of only one kind of corn—field—and that was the corn used both for the stock and for our table. We had it fried for breakfast, in pudding, stewed, and later in the season roasted in the oven. It would be slightly brown, crispy, chewy, and delicious.

The first hams of the season would be cooked about July and August in case an unexpected summer guest dropped in. Ham held the same rating as the basic black dress. If you had a ham in the meat house any situation could be faced. On short notice, it would be sliced and fried with special red gravy. Otherwise, it would be leisurely simmered, then defatted and browned. The smoked shoulder was indispensable as a seasoning for other meat dishes; a slice would be added in to fried chicken, guinea fowl, rabbit, squirrel, or quail. It was used also in boiled pots of cabbage, beans, watercress, and green black-eyed peas.

Besides these memorable summer dishes, it was always a great treat to make ice cream on a hot summer afternoon. Mother invariably made a custard-base ice cream and sometimes she would scorch the custard, which gave the ice cream an interesting flavor that still lingers in my younger brother's memory, so he tells me. But first we had to fetch the ice from the icehouse at Lahore. Ice was as novel to us as the ice cream itself. The nearest thing we had to a refrigerator was a box that we set in the spring; it had an opening in each end to let the water pass through and there we would put our milk, butter, and other perishables. Once we got the ice the afternoon would be taken up with chipping it and turning the freezer; it was a 5-gallon freezer and required lots of turns. When the ice cream was done, the dasher would be removed and we would lick the cream off it immediately. The cream in the freezer had to sit a while to congeal. Once I remember looking into the freezer can the next morning and finding that the leftover ice cream had all returned to milk. It was like the disappearance of Cinderella's new clothes.

Another late afternoon feast would be the melons my father had gathered in the early morning from the melon patch while the dew still lingered on them. He would put them in a tub of water or underneath the shrubbery until we were ready to eat them. Before he ever sliced open a melon, he would always plug it—by cutting out a small piece which he would taste to see if it had the proper flavor. If it didn't, he would cast it aside until he found a good one. We would all be served in our turn and we would enjoy each bite, discussing which condiment made the melon even sweeter—salt or pepper. After the feast, the rinds were saved and made into pickle or preserve, and the rest went into the swill for the hogs. Then we would go off to do our evening chores.

AN EARLY SUMMER BREAKFAST

Ham in Heavy Cream Sauce
Covered Fried Eggs
Pan-Fried Sweet Potatoes
Biscuits
Butter
Green Tomato Preserves
Coffee

Ham in Heavy Cream Sauce

Ham in heavy cream sauce was the most delicious combination one could ever hope to taste in leftovers. After carving away all the nice slices, the base of the ham was left with a lot of rough pieces. These were cut into 1-inch sizes and put into a saucepan containing heavy cream. The cream, which was skimmed from a crock of milk two days old, was much heavier than what we know as heavy cream, which is separated by a machine at the time of milking. The ham and cream mixture was then set on the back of the stove to heat without even reaching a simmer. When ready, the sauce would be thick and flavored by the pieces of ham—no other flavor added. It was served with hot biscuits or, if one liked, spooned over an open-faced biscuit. If you are having a Virginia ham you can still use the broken pieces, but not the bottom of the ham because that is usually dry and stringy. I don't think any other type of ham is any good. They just don't have the same flavor.

1 cup cut-up ham
2 cups heavy cream

Serves 4 to 5

Heat the cream to a scald, add the ham pieces, mix lightly, and set the saucepan on a low burner. The ham and cream mixture will more or less dry out in about ½ hour. Remove from the burner and serve piping hot.

Covered Fried Eggs

Covered fried eggs were developed by women who loved the outdoors and were anxious to get into the field or flower garden. When the meat was about ready in the oven and the coffee and the bread were all ready, a big skillet was set on the hot section of the stove—that is, over the fire box. Some fat from cooking bacon was added and when the pan began to smoke, a dozen eggs were broken one by one and carefully slipped in. A cover was placed on top. When the rest of the food was served up, the eggs were ready, beautiful, and looked as if they had been poached. They were placed upon a platter and decorated with delicious crisp bacon, or placed surrounding the ham.

Pan-Fried Sweet Potatoes

Fried sweet potatoes were as popular as white and the flavor always seemed enhanced by frying. We enjoyed them most served for breakfast or with a light supper. Sometimes they were boiled, left overnight, then peeled, sliced, and sautéed in butter. But they had a different taste from the ones that were peeled raw and sliced, and that was the way they were more often cooked.

1½ to 2 pounds sweet potatoes or yams   *Serves 4 to 5*
5 tablespoons butter

It is better to purchase large potatoes. They make a nice slice. They can be sliced on the bias or in a round slice ⅛ inch thick. Heat a 9- or 12-inch heavy skillet. Add butter and when the foaming stage is reached toss in the sweet potatoes. Cover and adjust the heat to avoid burning. After 4 to 5 minutes of cooking uncover and turn the potatoes over. Put the cover back on and cook until tender, another 4 to 5 minutes. Uncover and leave to dry out and most of the slices will become glazed and golden in color. Serve hot.

For recipe for **Biscuits,** see page 124.

For recipe for **Green Tomato Preserves,** see page 176.

AN EARLY SUMMER LUNCH

Potted Stuffed Squab

Buttered Green Beans

Steamed Lamb's-Quarters

Clover-Leaf Rolls

Butter

Brandied Peaches

Yellow Vanilla Pound Cake

Coffee

Potted Stuffed Squab

Squab was considered a rare delicacy. Mother somehow managed to find them when someone she thought special was coming to visit, particularly if the guest was an older person. In those days, the old were revered for their age and experience and treated with respect. Squabs were considered particularly good because they were most easily digested, even if we did cook them in loads of butter.

The squabs we eat are quite different from the pigeons we see around in city parks. They are specially raised and are killed just after their mothers stop feeding them, before they develop muscle from flying or pecking around on the ground. The meat is dark, tender, rich in flavor, and delightful eating. In cities, squab can be found in good butcher shops or ordered on request. You should allow one per person.

To prepare for cooking, singe off the pinfeathers that usually cover the squab. Wash inside and out with a clean cloth. It is the stuffing that is the real secret to making them taste delicious.

6 slices white bread, crust removed   *Serves 4*
1 cup milk
Liver from the squabs
Salt and pepper
4 tablespoons (¼ cup) melted butter
4 squabs
2 tablespoons soft butter
¼ teaspoon thyme
½ cup butter
Parsley

Place the slices of bread in a flat platter and pour the milk over. After a few minutes of soaking, pick up each slice of bread by hand and squeeze the milk out. Discard the milk and fluff the bread up by tearing it into small pieces. Break the liver into small bits and mix with the bread. Season with salt and pepper. Add melted butter, mix well, and stuff the cavity of each squab. Stitch the opening and tie the legs together. Rub it over with soft butter. Sprinkle over with salt, pepper, and thyme.

Take an iron pot and heat it hot. Add ½ cup of butter. When the foaming stage is reached, add the squabs. Sear well on all sides, cover, and turn the burner down low. Cook on the top of the stove, turning often during cooking. Cook for 1½ hours. If you prefer to roast in the oven, leave the birds uncovered and cook in a preheated 375° oven for 1 hour, basting often. When done, remove from the pot and place the squabs on a hot platter. Add a few drops of water to the juice in the pan, season to taste, and cook for a minute or two. Pour the sauce over the squab in the platter, garnish with parsley, and serve hot.

Buttered Green Beans

Early tender green beans were cooked and served buttered as a change from the more matured and meaty ones.

1½ pounds green beans   *Serves 5 to 6*
2 teaspoons salt
1½ tablespoons butter
1 teaspoon finely cut chervil

Rinse the beans and snip the ends off. Fill a 4-quart saucepan with cold water and bring to a rolling boil. Add salt and drop in green beans slowly to keep water boiling. When all of the beans are in, give them a stir to see that they all become blanched right away. While keeping the beans at a rolling boil, skim away any scum that arises on the surface of the pot. Cook uncovered for 10 minutes. Drain and cover. Keep on a warm spot. Heat butter to the foaming stage and pour over the beans. Sprinkle on chervil and a little salt if needed. Shake the pan around to see that all of the beans are buttered. Put the cover back on and hold for a few minutes while waiting for the rest of the meal to finish cooking.

Steamed Lamb's-Quarters

Lamb's-quarters grows bountifully from early spring through early fall in well-enriched spots such as gardens and truck patches (patches of field-grown vegetables). It is very much like spinach in taste and texture but without the acid aftertaste. It is delicious cooked with a meat stock or steamed in a colander and served with oil sprinkled over. And it is free for the gathering. As it grows old it is best to use the top or tip-end tender leaves. (As to amounts, that depends upon how much one can find in the field or garden.) We used to mix many different leafy greens together to make a potful, but the lamb's-quarters is delicious by itself.

All leafy green vegetables are at their tenderest in early spring and again in late fall when the hot sun of summer can no longer toughen their leaves.

1 gallon lamb's-quarters   *Serves 5*
1 quart water
½ pound cured meat, shoulder or cured, un-
    sliced bacon (optional)

Lamb's-quarters collapses like spinach after it is cooked. So although a gallon sounds like a lot, you will need that much; prepare a quart at a time if easier. Wash and drain leaves, put in a colander and set it over a pan of boiling water. After 3 minutes turn the leaves over and cook for another 2 minutes. Then remove them from the colander and place them in a dish.

To cook with meat: Boil smoked shoulder of pork in 1 quart of water for an hour. Remove the meat and add the washed and drained leaves to the boiling meat stock. Cook briskly, uncovered. Stir to see that all the leaves have been blanched by the boiling stock. Cook for 10 minutes, drain, and serve hot or set aside until the rest of the meal is ready.

Note: When using seasoned meats, usually you don't need to add salt. The most desirable meats are smoke-cured; we never used fat-back and salt pork because they are not as flavorsome.

Clover-Leaf Rolls

Clover-leaf rolls are made from the same dough as the yeast rolls. Although bread made in different shapes from the same dough has a seemingly different taste and texture, clover-leaf rolls were served when we wanted the bread to be more attractive-looking on the bread plate. The rolls are made by pinching off four small balls the size of quarters from the yeast dough (page 11) after it has risen. Butter each ball, then place all four in one of the cups of a 12-cup muffin tin. Repeat until all the cups in the tin have been filled. Place the pan in a draft-free place of 80° to 90° until the dough rises to the top or doubles. Set the rolls into a preheated 375° oven to bake for about 20 minutes. Remove from the oven and leave in the pan a few minutes to rest before serving.

Brandied Peaches

A recipe for brandied peaches would have been better given by my Aunt Jenny Hailstalk, an elegant lady and a masterful cook, who envied no one. Her kitchen and vegetable garden were always orderly and her flowers were beautiful—scented geraniums filling the air with their fragrance. Her only child, a son, grew up and left for the city. We were left to visit and enjoy her store of knowledge and experience. Being a warm, friendly person, her friends were many and her table was always set. It was usually covered with three tiers of tablecloths, the first one touching the floor.

She and her husband were great farmers. Like the other people of Freetown they raised crops, stock, and poultry. Everyone else had either a well house or a milk house. They had both. The well house was a latticework structure, whitewashed with lime. The walls inside were lined with shelves containing perishable delicacies, all being preserved by the cool air coming up from the well. It was in the well house that she kept her brandied peaches.

Preparing peaches in Aunt Jenny's day was quite a task. First of all, peaches were very deliciously sweet and covered with a kind of wool or fur. To prepare them for brandying she would drop the peaches for a few minutes into a pot of boiling hot water containing a small quantity of lye—it helped to remove the fuzz from the peaches. Lye was used quite a lot in the preparation of food, as well as for making soap for household use. After a minute or two in the lye water, she would quickly dip them out and rub them with a clean, coarse cloth, removing the fur and some of the skin of the peach. Then she would wash them in cold water and dry them. She placed them in a stone jar, alternating layers of brown sugar and peaches until the jar was filled. Finally, she poured old brandy over them and tied the jar over with a strong, clean cloth and left them to age until needed.

I can remember her company dinners when she served the brandied peaches with thin slices of her famous yellow vanilla pound cake, something she usually kept on hand on the sideboard. Sometimes she served brandied peaches as an accompaniment to meat dishes, especially ham and game.

The fur has been bred out of peaches today, as well as most of their flavor. However, brandied peaches are still delicious and can be made without being dipped in lye solution. I still prefer fruit that has not been sprayed. It is well to use bottled water, if you live in an area where the water is highly chlorinated, in order to get the best out of the select fruit you are preserving.

Makes 8 1-quart jars

> 4 pounds light-brown sugar (not brownulated)
> 2 cups bottled water
> 7 pounds select peaches (sound, without
>   blemishes, and flavorful)
> 1 quart brandy
>
> *8 1-quart jars*

Into a wide-bottomed, good-quality, stainless pot, pour the sugar and water. Let set until the sugar has dissolved, then cook gently for 10 minutes. In the meantime, wash the peaches and rub them dry, removing any fur. Place the peaches in the kettle of sugar syrup in their skins. Cook gently until tender when pierced with a pointed toothpick (about 30 minutes). Do not overcook. Remove from the burner when just tender, then, with a slotted spoon, remove the peaches from the syrup and place them on a platter in a single layer. Return the syrup to the burner and cook until the syrup is reduced by one third. Add an equal amount of good brandy to the reduced syrup, heat hot, and add the peaches (discard the syrup left on the platter). When the peaches and syrup become hot but not boiling, have ready sterilized jars sitting in boiling water. Fill up with the peaches and pour over enough syrup to cover the peach at the top of the jar. Try to gently press the top peaches under the shoulder of the jar and fill within a fraction of the top. It is best to use jars with glass tops and wire clamps to hold them sealed. Wipe the top rim of the jar before placing the rubber ring on it. Remove the jars of fruit from the hot water and set in a draft-free place until cool. Store in a cool, dark place.

Yellow Vanilla Pound Cake

The keeping quality of pound cake made it a popular favorite, plus the fact that the main ingredients were always available: butter, eggs, and flour. Sugar and flavoring were nearby at Lahore store. All the grownups had their own way of measuring, be it on a dime, nickel, teacup, or sifter, and their cakes were perfect. It was my dream to make a pound cake to equal theirs. I learned that the formula for a good pound cake is a slow oven, cold butter, carefully measured flour (too much flour will cause the cake to crack on top), and proper mixing of butter, sugar, and eggs.

1 cup (½ pound) cold butter
1⅔ cups sugar
¼ teaspoon salt
5 eggs (medium to large, but not jumbo)
2 cups sifted unbleached flour
1 tablespoon vanilla extract
1 teaspoon fresh-squeezed lemon juice

1 9-inch tube pan

Put the butter in a large mixing bowl and work it with a wooden spoon until it becomes shiny, about 5 minutes. Add in the sugar and salt and continue to work sugar and butter together. When well mixed, begin to stir in a circular motion until the mixture loses most of the gritty feeling. The addition of eggs will dissolve the rest. Add eggs one at a time, stirring well after each addition. After the third egg has been incorporated add 2 tablespoons of flour and stir well. This will keep the batter from separating. Add the fourth and fifth egg and continue to stir, then the rest of the flour in four parts, stirring well after each addition. Finally beat in the vanilla and lemon juice. Butter and dust tube pan on the bottom only; the sides should remain ungreased because the cake will adhere to the sides better when rising. Spoon the batter into the pan. Set into an oven that has been preheated long enough for the heat to have risen and become stable at between 275° and 300°. Bake for 40 minutes at that temperature, then raise the temperature to 325° for 20 minutes. Remove from oven, run a knife around the sides of the pan, turn out right away on a wire rack and turn face up. Cool uncovered for 15 minutes, then cover with a clean towel, otherwise the cake will become dry and hard. When cold, store in a clean tin. Plastic containers develop an undesirable odor.

Note: Two teaspoons of almond extract can be used in place of lemon and vanilla.

AN EARLY SUMMER DINNER

Sautéed Veal Kidney

Skillet Scallions

Spoon Bread

Butter

Salad of Simpson Lettuce and Young Beet Tops

Strawberries and Cream

Sponge Cake

Coffee

Scallions, like asparagus, are a wonderful spring vegetable and they are a good change. They are tempting to look at, have a mild and interesting flavor, and they go particularly well with veal kidneys, as well as with mutton, steak, and chops. And this was the season when strawberries were plentiful.

Sautéed Veal Kidney

3 veal kidneys   *Serves 5*
5 tablespoons butter
2 slices bacon, chopped
¼ cup wine, white or red
Fresh-ground black pepper
Salt
2 teaspoons chopped chervil

Kidneys are better if purchased in the fat because they stay fresh longer and are kept from drying out. Try to get them that way. To open, take a sharp knife and cut lengthwise through the fat to the kidney, cutting away the nerves and the thin skin that covers the kidney. (Sometimes the skin comes off with the fat.) Cut the kidney in half lengthwise and slice across, making ¼-inch slices along the bias. Heat a 12-inch skillet with 2 tablespoons of the butter. When the pan is hot add the cubed bacon and render the fat from it. Then remove the pieces and pour off the fat. Add the remaining butter to the residue left in the skillet; when hot but not burning, add the slices of kidneys. Sauté only enough to heat each piece through, about 3 to 4 minutes. Remove the slices from the pan with a slotted spoon and place them on a serving platter. Then add the wine to the sauce left in the skillet and simmer a minute or two. Sprinkle pepper, salt, and the pieces of bacon over the kidneys. Pour the chopped chervil over the hot sauce.

Note: We always saved the suet from the kidney, cut it into small pieces, and rendered it. The fat was excellent for frying doughnuts and using in general.

Skillet Scallions

4 bunches scallions   *Serves 5*
3 tablespoons butter

Prepare the scallions by picking off any yellow stems. Cut away the fibrous roots from the bottom. Wash in cold water under tap, then cut the tops down to fit the skillet. Heat the skillet and add the butter. When the foaming stage is reached, put in the scallions. The few drops of water left on the scallions from washing are enough for steaming. Cover the skillet and cook over a moderate fire. Turn them over after about 3 minutes. Total cooking time is about 4 to 5 minutes. Be careful not to overcook; the white part should be a bit crisp, the tops tender, shiny, and green. No salt or pepper will be needed.

Spoon Bread

1 cup water-ground white cornmeal   *Serves 5*
½ teaspoon salt
2 teaspoons sugar
⅓ teaspoon baking soda
2 teaspoons Royal Baking Powder
3 medium-sized eggs, beaten
3 tablespoons butter
2 cups buttermilk

1 8 x 8 x 2-inch baking pan, or a 1½-quart
  soufflé dish

Preheat oven to 400°. Sift the cornmeal, salt, sugar, soda, and baking powder together into a mixing bowl. Make a well in the center and add the beaten eggs. At this time put the butter in the baking pan and set it in the oven to heat. Stir the eggs into the meal vigorously, then pour in the buttermilk, stirring well again. Remove the hot pan from the oven and tilt it around to butter the entire surface. Pour the excess butter into the meal batter, stir quickly, and pour the batter into the hot baking dish. Bake for 35 minutes in a 400° oven. Serve in the pan right from the oven with loads of fresh butter.

For recipe for **Salad of Simpson Lettuce and Young Beet Tops,** see page 10.

Strawberries and Cream

As children we looked forward eagerly to the ripening of wild strawberries, searching along fence rows and in fields along streams for the berries. It was unbelievable that anything so delicious could ripen so early in spring. They were fleeting—in a week they would appear and then be gone. Many of the wild berries around us were as large as the cultivated ones and we would sort them out to serve fresh with a pitcher of delicious cream. The smaller ones were made into preserves (see page 22) and usually served at breakfast with hot biscuits. We were not allowed to indulge in sugar except on special occasions, so it would be a beautiful day in spring when we sat down before a bowl of strawberries and cream. The milk was allowed to set for 2 to 3 days for the cream to fully rise to the top. It was the consistency of a smooth sour cream with loads of sugar added.

Sponge Cake

5 eggs (medium to large, but not jumbo)
1 cup very fine sugar

1 tablespoon vanilla extract
2 teaspoons fresh lemon juice
¾ cup flour
1 teaspoon salt

1 9-inch tube pan

Separate the eggs and beat the yolks in a mixing bowl until they are a bright-lemon color. Add the sugar gradually and continue beating until the mixture forms ribbons when the spoon is held above the bowl. Then add the vanilla and lemon. Beat the egg whites until they form firm, but not hard, peaks. Fold the egg whites into the yolk mixture, then alternate, sifting some of the flour and salt into the batter. Continue to fold and sift in the flour until it is used up. Spoon the batter into a 9-inch ungreased tube pan with false bottom. It is important for sponge cake to adhere to the walls of the pan. Set in a preheated 350° oven for 40 minutes. Remove the pan from the oven and immediately place it face down upon a wire rack and let the cake hang for about 40 minutes before setting it upright again. This process keeps the cake from collapsing during the cooling period and also holds the texture of the cake. Remove the cake from the pan and place it in a tin that is not completely airtight, otherwise a sweat will develop. Sponge cake is best cut with a serrated knife, using a sawing motion, or pulled apart with two table forks.

Note: One tablespoon of sherry can be substituted for vanilla and lemon as flavoring.

A PREPARED-AHEAD SUMMER DINNER

Steamed Chicken in Casserole

Wilted Lettuce with Hot Vinegar Dressing

Thin-Sliced Cucumbers Marinated in Sugar and White Vinegar

Sliced Yeast Bread

Butter

Blueberry Cake with Blueberry Sauce

Coffee

Spring and early summer outdoor activity called for meals that could be made without spending too much time in the kitchen. Dishes like steamed chicken could be set on the back of the stove or in the oven, allowing everyone to enjoy working outside.

Steamed Chicken in Casserole

This recipe can be quickly made and cooked without too much watching.

Serves 4 to 5

1 2½-pound chicken with a few extra wings
½ cup (1 stick) butter
2 medium-sized onions, chopped fine

¼ teaspoon thyme
1 bay leaf
½ cup sliced carrots
½ tablespoon chopped fresh tarragon
Salt and pepper

Have the chicken cut into 8 pieces. Wash off and dry with a clean cloth. Into a heavy pot or saucepan put the butter and heat to the foaming stage. Add the onions. When the onions are quite heated through, add in the chicken. Raise the flame and brown the chicken and onions well, without burning. When the chicken is well browned, turn the burner as low as possible, add the thyme, bay leaf, and carrots, cover with a closely fitting lid, and simmer for 1½ hours. Stir by shaking the pot around. The pot can be set into a preheated 250° oven. Be sure it's quite hot when set into the oven. Cook for 45 minutes. If you have fresh tarragon add ½ tablespoon about 15 minutes before removing from the oven, then salt and pepper to taste, and swish the pot around to blend in the herb. Adding the tarragon at the last gives a better flavor than if it is cooked in from the beginning. Don't use dried tarragon; it is too strong. The chicken wings can be removed if you like; they are added really to give thickness to the sauce, which comes from the two last wing joints.

Wilted Lettuce with Hot Vinegar Dressing

Wilted lettuce was served as a vegetable during the period between spring and summer when there wasn't too much from the garden. The lettuce leaves were washed, crisped, drained dry, and put into a bowl. Then they were seared in a combination of bacon fat, vinegar, and sugar that was boiled up and poured over the lettuce; then sprinkled with finely chopped bacon. For this dish we used Simpson or Grand Rapids lettuce, but iceberg lettuce would be good.

1 head iceberg lettuce   *Serves 4 to 5*
3 slices bacon
1 teaspoon sugar
¼ cup vinegar

Remove the outer leaves, using the inside crisp ones. Leave the smaller ones whole. Break away from the stem and reassemble the head loosely in a bowl. Fry 3 slices of good-flavored bacon, then remove the bacon and most of the fat, leaving about 2 tablespoons of fat and residue from the bacon. Now add the sugar and vinegar; bring to a boil, swishing the pan around to stir. Pour this boiling mixture over the lettuce in the bowl. Crumble up the bacon and scatter over the top. Serve while piping hot.

Thin-Sliced Cucumbers with White Vinegar Dressing

Cucumbers grew abundantly in our garden all summer, and we enjoyed them every day during the season. We always served them in a very sweet and peppery dressing.

3 medium-sized tender cucumbers   *Serves 4 to 5*
1 teaspoon salt
⅔ cup white vinegar
½ cup sugar
1 teaspoon finely cut chervil
⅛ teaspoon pepper

Wash cucumbers, leaving rind on if they have not been sprayed or waxed, and slice very thin with a sharp paring knife. Put the sliced pieces into a deep bowl. Sprinkle them with the salt. Mix a bit and set a heavy bowl on top of the cucumbers with a weight in it so that the cucumbers release their water. Put everything in the refrigerator. After the cucumbers have been sitting an hour or more, remove them from the refrigerator and drain off the water. Mix the vinegar and sugar together until the sugar dissolves. Add to the cucumbers, sprinkle over with finely cut chervil, and return to the refrigerator until needed.

Yeast Bread

Loaf bread can be made from the same dough as the yeast rolls by pinching off about a quarter of the dough (see page 11). After buttering it over with a mixture of butter and lard, place it in a loaf pan, set it in an 80°-to-90° spot, and let it rise until it doubles in size. It should be at the top of the pan. Set the risen dough into a preheated 375° oven to bake for 30 minutes. Remove from the oven and let it rest in the pan a few minutes to soak, as they used to say, then turn out to cool.

If you plan to make the whole batch of dough into loaves, add a cup of whole-wheat flour for texture, substituting it for 1 cup of the white flour.

Blueberry Cake with Blueberry Sauce

Blueberry cake was a surprisingly good, quick dessert made at the last minute. When canning, there was always some leftover fruit that was not enough to fill a jar and it was usually used for the next meal to make a pudding, pie, plain compote, or blueberry cake.

2 cups sifted unbleached flour
¼ teaspoon salt
4 tablespoons butter
1 egg
1 cup milk
2 teaspoons vanilla
3 teaspoons Royal Baking Powder
1½ cups stewed blueberries
⅓ cup sugar
¼ teaspoon cinnamon

Serves 4 to 5
(with leftovers)

1 8 x 8 x 2-inch buttered baking pan

Sift the flour and salt into a mixing bowl. Add the butter and blend with fingertips or, even better, with a pastry blender until the mixture becomes grainy, fine, and a bit more coarse than cornmeal. Beat the egg and mix in the milk, then add to the dough, stirring all the while. Add the vanilla and continue stirring, then last, add the baking powder. Mix well and spoon into a well-buttered baking pan. Drain the blueberries and quickly scatter them over the dough. Combine the sugar and cinnamon and sprinkle over the top. Set the cake into a preheated 425° oven. Close the door and turn the oven down to 375°. Cook for 25 to 28 minutes.

Note: Draining the juice from the berries is to keep the cake from becoming too soggy while cooking. If using fresh berries, stew them for 3 to 4 minutes before putting on the dough. Drain away the juice and make into a sauce by boiling the juice, adding sugar to taste, and a teaspoon of cornstarch dissolved in a little cold water.

MIDSUMMER SUNDAY BREAKFAST

Virginia Fried Chicken with Browned Gravy

Sausage Cakes

Fried New Cymlings

Fried Green Corn

Biscuits

Corn Muffins

Damson Preserves

Coffee

The most pleasant memories come to my mind of a midsummer's breakfast. Windows and doors were flung open wide. Our bare feet had become completely toughened and comfortable as we sat and quietly relaxed on a long bench behind the table where a platter of hot fried chicken rested, along with fried vegetables such as corn or cymlings, sausage cakes, biscuits, batter bread or cornmeal muffins, jelly or preserves, coffee, and well water or milk for the children.

Virginia Fried Chicken with Browned Gravy

In Freetown, fried chicken was a very special dish. Like many other things of that day, frying chickens were produced only once a year in late spring through early summer. They were hand-raised and specially fed—producing the most delicious-flavored chicken. We fried them in sweet, home-rendered lard, churned butter, and a sliced piece of smoked ham for added flavor. The first fried chickens were served at Sunday morning breakfast when the outside work was finished. It was leisurely enjoyed with hot biscuits and delicious browned gravy.

> 1 cup all-purpose unbleached flour   *Serves 5 to 6*
> 1 cup whole-wheat flour
> 3 teaspoons salt
> 1 teaspoon fresh-ground black pepper
> 2 2¼- to 2½-pound chickens cut into 8 pieces
>   each
> ½ cup lard, at room temperature
> ½ cup (1 stick) butter, at room temperature
> 1 slice smoked ham (optional)

Combine the two flours and add the salt and pepper. Mix well. After the chickens have been rinsed off and cut into serving pieces (if not purchased precut), wipe them lightly with a damp cloth. Reserve backs and wing tips for the stock, which should be started at this point (see GRAVY directions below). Roll each piece of chicken in the flour mixture and place the coated pieces on a wide platter or a sheet of wax paper. Leave the floured pieces to rest for an hour or so to allow time for the flour to adhere to the chicken, avoiding loose flour falling into the frying pan and burning before the chicken pieces have a chance to brown properly.

   To fry the chicken, heat the skillet hot and add lard. When lard is nearly hot enough to begin smoking, add in chicken pieces and butter and optional ham. Chicken is better cooked on a brisk flame, but don't burn. It must be watched closely. The cooking fat should come halfway up the chicken in the pan so that when the pieces are turned over the whole piece will be evenly browned and thoroughly cooked. When all pieces are placed in the pan, cover and cook on a brisk fire. Cook each side to a good golden color, 10 to 12 minutes on each side. It can be turned a number of times to get the desired brown color. I find a heavy-bottomed aluminum pan is excellent for frying chicken. The black iron pan is good on a wood stove that has a wider heating surface. The total cooking time should not be much more than 25 minutes. Because chickens today are reared mostly in confinement, they are very tender and don't need long cooking. Remove the cooked pieces from the skillet, drain on a paper towel, and serve piping hot with gravy.

GRAVY

3 chicken backs, any wing tips and feet
1 stalk celery with leaves
1 thick slice onion
3 cups cold water
4 tablespoons fat from chicken pan
3 rounded tablespoons flour
Salt and pepper

Prepare the stock in advance with the chicken backs, celery, onion, and water in a saucepan. Put on a medium burner to cook for 1 hour, gently but continuously. When cooked enough, strain and set aside to cool and skim off the fat. When the chicken is halfway through cooking, spoon out about 4 or 5 tablespoons of fat from the pan in which it is cooking into a 9-inch skillet; add the flour and set over a medium flame. Stir until the pan heats up and the flour turns a dark chestnut brown. Remove the skillet from the burner and add in 2½ cups chicken stock. Stir well and return the skillet to the burner. Bring to a simmer and cook gently for 15 minutes. Season to taste with salt and pepper. If gravy is too thick, add more stock or plain water. Remove any excess fat that rises on top of gravy and serve hot along with the fried chicken.

Rendering Lard from Pork Fat

For a special meal with hot biscuits and fried chicken, try rendering some lard for that special occasion. Ask your butcher for some clean, fresh pork leaf fat or pieces cut from the loin. Sometimes it is found in supermarkets. Two pounds of fat will make enough for both the biscuits and to fry the chicken in.

To prepare the fat, first cut away any lean part. Wipe or scrape off any residue from the butcher's block and cut the fat in 1-inch pieces of equal size; otherwise, some pieces will brown before others. Place ½ cup water in a heavy-bottomed pot. This will prevent the fat from burning before it begins to melt. Cook on a medium-high burner, stirring constantly until the fat begins to melt. When the fat is halfway into the cooking, lower the flame so as to prevent burning. When the cracklings become brown and begin floating, they are nearly finished. Continue to stir throughout. Keep lowering the flame to prevent the fat from burning. When all the cracklings are brown and floating, strain the fat into a heatproof bowl. This fat is very hot; be careful not to get scalded or spill any fat on the stove. It is almost like liquid fuel. Strain the defatted pieces through a sieve and save for crackling bread or discard.

Fresh home-rendered lard makes the most perfect, beautifully browned biscuits and the same goes for fried chicken. Store the lard in a clean, dry container, cover, and keep in the refrigerator. It lasts months.

Sausage Cakes

After hog butchering, many pounds of sausage were ground and preserved in various ways for keeping during the short period the sausage lasted. Some was encased in pork intestines and smoked, giving a flavor that men liked. A good quantity was baked in loaf pans and sealed over with lots of fat and set in the meat house to keep cold. The rest was made into small cakes, fried in a good quantity of fresh rendered lard, and canned in glass jars. When the jars had cooled a bit they were turned upside down so that the fat could fill up the top and neck of the jar, blocking out any air that otherwise would seep into the jar under the rubber ring. This was the only way one could keep sausage from spoiling at that time. When the weather warmed up the jars were set, still resting on the tops, into the meat house on the dirt floor to keep until summer and the sausages were served on special occasions. They held well and kept their delicious flavor and texture. When we were ready to use a jar, we would set it in warm water to melt the fat, then open it up and remove the cakes. They were placed in the oven to heat through and served hot.

There is a recipe for making sausage on page 206. Let the flavor ripen a few days before cooking them.

Fried New Cymlings

In summer when fruits, garden and field vegetables were ripening, succulent dishes of the season's first would be served at breakfast. Usually, fried new corn sliced from the cob; tart summer apples; eggplant, sliced and pressed overnight, dipped in batter, fried crispy; fried tomatoes sprinkled with brown sugar; and, most delicate of all, cymling, a squash of delicate flavor, picked while very tender, sliced and fried, a delicious accompaniment to breakfast bacon.

Cymlings can be found in the city markets in late summer and fall and are a refreshing change from the usual summer squashes.

2 pounds cymlings   *Serves 5 to 6*
4 tablespoons clean bacon fat
Salt and pepper
1 teaspoon sugar

To prepare, wash the cymlings, wipe dry, and slice into ¼-inch wedges. Spill the cymlings into a hot skillet containing 4 tablespoons of clean bacon fat. Cover and cook briskly without burning for 10 minutes. Cook uncovered another 12 minutes over a medium heat, sprinkle with salt and pepper and a teaspoon of sugar. Set aside until ready to serve. Reheat and serve hot.

Fried Green Corn

6 ears corn   *Serves 5 to 6*
2 tablespoons fresh bacon fat or butter
½ teaspoon salt
2 teaspoons sugar
¼ teaspoon black pepper

Slice the corn from the cob. Scrape the cob downward to get any remaining corn left near the cob. Heat a 9-inch skillet and add the fat. When hot, spoon in the corn and cook for 15 to 20 minutes, stirring often. While cooking, sprinkle in salt, sugar, and pepper. Serve piping hot.

For recipe for **Biscuits,** see page 124.

Corn Muffins

1 to 2 tablespoons lard
2½ cups water-ground white cornmeal
1 scant teaspoon salt
1 teaspoon baking soda
½ teaspoon Royal Baking Powder
2 cups sour milk
1 egg, well-beaten
2 tablespoons melted butter

Makes 1 dozen

1 12-cup muffin tin

Grease muffin tin generously with lard and set in a 400° oven. Pans for cooking corn batter should always be piping hot. Sift the corn-meal, salt, soda, and baking powder into a mixing bowl. Add in the sour milk and stir well. Add the beaten egg and the melted butter. Fill each cup and place in a preheated 400° oven. Bake for 20 to 25 minutes. Serve hot with lots of butter.

For recipe for **Damson Preserves,** see page 157.

A BUSY-DAY SUMMER DINNER

Chicken Gelatine

Pork-Seasoned Rape

Boiled New Onions

Sliced Tomatoes with Special Seasoning

Assorted Breads from Breakfast

Butter

Wild Blackberry Jelly

Compote of Stewed Blackberries

Busy-Day Cake or Sugar Cookies

Coffee

The preparation of a meal on a busy summer day, of which there were many, began before breakfast. The salad greens, vegetables, and berries were gathered while the dew was still on them. Chicken gelatine was a simple way to prepare a delicious dish for a hot and busy day, getting the chicken started on the back of the stove while breakfast cooked. A busy-day cake, or sweet bread, as it was really called, was regular cake batter, measured out and stirred in a hurry while the vegetables cooked on one end of the old wood stove and canning was carried out on the firebox end. The batter would be poured into a large biscuit pan and set into the oven to bake. Or we would have sugar cookies that had been already made on a more leisurely day. Our busiest days were, of course, when we were canning, putting up watermelon-rind pickles and Seckel pears, making blackberry jelly, and preparing the brine for cucumber pickles.

Chicken Gelatine

1 3- to 3½-pound chicken   *Serves 4 to 5*
Salt and fresh-ground pepper to taste
¼ teaspoon freshly chopped or dried thyme
4 tablespoons (½ stick) soft butter
8 tablespoons (1 stick) butter

Take a plump chicken, wash it inside and out with cold water, and wipe dry with a clean cloth. Remove the wings with a good, sharp knife. This will help the chicken to brown and cook evenly. Rub the chicken inside with salt, pepper, and thyme. Put 4 tablespoons soft butter inside the chicken. Tie the legs together. Do not season the outside. In an oval pot large enough to hold the chicken heat 8 tablespoons butter. When the butter reaches the foaming stage, put in the chicken and the wings. Sear the chicken well all over, but see that it does not burn. Don't worry about browning the chicken; that will develop with long cooking. Cover well and cook on a very low burner for at least 2 hours. It is most important that the casserole does not boil, but that the chicken simmers in the butter and its own sauce without a drop of water being added. After about 40 to 45 minutes, liquid will develop in the pot. Drain it into a bowl; if allowed to cook it will evaporate and be lost. Baste the chicken every 20 minutes or so with the fat from the broth in the bowl. Continue to cook and baste, removing the liquid as it develops. When the chicken is cooked, remove it to a platter. Skim fat from the broth in the bowl and pour the broth back into the pan that the chicken was cooked in. Heat the contents gently, running a spoon around the pan, dislodging any particles adhering to the pan. Simmer lightly, season, and strain into the platter around the chicken. Leave to cool until suppertime. By this time, the broth will have jelled.

The flavor of the chicken cooked this way is unbelievably delicious, buttery and sweet without the use of salt and pepper.

Sometimes smaller chickens were used, split in half and cooked in the same manner.

Two chickens can be done in a larger casserole.

Pork-Seasoned Rape

Each region had its own particular leafy green vegetable. The one most cultivated in our area was rape, a bluish-green plant, smooth to the touch, and very much like a young cabbage plant. It was rather brittle, tender, and not as bitter as some of the other leafy greens. Its good feature was that it could be planted very early, developed and grown throughout the cool spring season. The seeds were sown again in early August and lasted until late fall. Rape, lamb's-quarters, and wild watercress were all cooked in the same manner: boiled or steamed in a broth that had been cooked with a piece of smoked pork. Certain parts of the pork were especially selected for boiling, particularly the shoulder, being a cut with less fat and quite bony. It was the flavor of the meat and not the fat that seasoned the broth, unless it was fat from boiled ham. There is no kind of pork that seasons or gives flavor to a boiled pot of leafy greens or beans as does smoked pork.

Early in the morning a piece of pork was put to boil while breakfast was being prepared. The rape would be picked with the dew still upon it while breakfast cooked. Later in the morning the greens were picked over and washed, the meat removed from the pot, and the greens cooked in the broth. Then they would be set aside to be served at midday dinner. At that time they were reheated and served.

Serves 4 to 5

½ to 1 pound pork, preferably smoked shoulder
1 quart water
2½ to 3 pounds rape

Cook the pork and water in a ½-gallon pot for an hour and a half or more, until the meat is completely tender. When done, remove the piece of pork and add the rape, using as much as 3 pounds. Pack it into the pot, since it shrinks as it is heated. Cook until tender, which should be in 15 to 20 minutes. Remove from the burner until ready to serve. When ready to serve, reheat and drain the liquid off. Serve hot.

Boiled New Onions

One usually thinks of boiled onions only at Thanksgiving and Christmas, but we served them throughout the year. They were planted in late winter and thinned out as they grew. In the scallion stage they were used in many ways—fried with tops included, braised and sliced very thin and added to a lettuce salad of vinegar and sugar. Later in the season, when a bulb of about 1 inch in diameter had developed, they were boiled just enough to be tender yet crisp, and served dotted with butter and a sprinkling of chervil or parsley.

Sliced Tomatoes with Special Seasoning

There were high points of the summer that made your work rewarding. One was the day you picked the first ripe tomato. From that day until the first frost, no dinner was complete without a dish of sliced luscious red tomatoes, sprinkled liberally with granulated sugar and fresh black pepper with a light touch of salt, then left to marinate for 10 to 15 minutes. It was a marriage of flavors that needed no other touches except perhaps a garnish of chervil, the common herb of my childhood.

Compote of Stewed Blackberries

Everyone seems to have forgotten how delicious blackberries were—
if they ever knew. We picked them mainly for canning, for making
wine and jelly to use in the winter, but how we did enjoy them too
during the summer season in blackberry pie, rolypoly, or with cream
and sugar, as well as stewed and served warm. Blackberries are still
gathered from the wild and they are the one frozen fruit that still
tastes good. Put up in Marion, Oregon, they can be purchased in the
A & P frozen, and they are just delicious when stewed for 10 minutes with a little water and sugar to taste. Serve warm with cookies
or cold with warm, plain cake.

> 1 cup sugar   *Serves 4 to 5*
> 1 cup well water or bottled water
> 1 pint blackberries

Set the sugar and water to boil briskly for 10 to 12 minutes. Pick
over the berries, wash them off, and drain on a clean towel. Then
add them to the boiled syrup. Bring this to a near boil and stew
gently for 10 minutes. Turn the heat off and leave in a warm spot
if they are to be served warm.

Busy-Day Cake or Sweet Bread

Busy-day cake was never iced, it was always cut into squares and
served warm, often with fruit or berries left over from canning. The
delicious flavor of fresh-cooked fruit with the plain cake was just to
our taste and it was also refreshing with newly churned, chilled buttermilk or cold morning's milk.

Serves 4 to 5
(with leftovers)

8 tablespoons (1 stick) butter, at room temperature
1⅓ cups granulated sugar
3 medium to large eggs
2 cups sifted flour
½ cup sweet milk, at room temperature
¼ teaspoon salt
2 teaspoons vanilla
4 teaspoons Royal Baking Powder
1 light grating of nutmeg (about 25 grains)

1 10 x 10 x 2-inch cake pan

Blend the butter and sugar by hand until it is light and fluffy. Then, one by one, add the eggs, beating the batter with a wooden spoon after each egg. Add in ½ cup of flour and one part of the milk, alternating the milk in three parts and the flour in four parts, and ending with the flour. Add salt, vanilla, baking powder, and nutmeg, and mix well. Stir well after each addition, but always stir only once after you have added milk, then quickly add more flour so as to keep the batter from separating.

Butter and flour the bottom of the cake pan and spoon the batter into it. Bake in a preheated 375° oven for 40 minutes. Cut into squares and serve warm.

Sugar Cookies

2 cups granulated sugar
1 cup butter
2 eggs, beaten
4 cups sifted flour
½ cup sour milk or buttermilk
1 level teaspoon baking soda
¼ teaspoon salt
½ teaspoon nutmeg (optional)
2 cups crushed cube sugar

*Makes about
40 cookies*

Blend the granulated sugar and butter together in a bowl, using your hands for mixing. Add beaten eggs and stir well by hand. Add half the flour and stir well. Pour in milk and the rest of the flour with the baking soda, salt, and nutmeg. Mix until smooth, spoon the dough onto a flat dish, and set to chill 3 to 4 hours. Then roll out on a well-dusted surface to about ¼-inch thickness. Cut out cookies with a 2-inch round cutter.

Crush the cube sugar with a mallet and put the sugar on a sheet of wax paper. Crushed cube sugar is better for topping than regular granulated. It has more body and makes a heavier topping. Now pick up the rounds of cookie dough and turn them face down into the sugar. Pick them up and place on a cookie sheet. The pressing into the sugar will increase the size of the cookie. We used to call them horse cakes, I think because of the size. Set the cookies to bake in a 375° oven for 5 to 7 minutes. Watch carefully to see that they don't brown too much. An overbrowned cookie loses its delicate flavor. Leave to cool on a wire rack and store in a dry tin.

PUTTING UP FRUITS AND VEGETABLES, PICKLES, AND WINE

Wild Blackberry Jelly

Here is how we made our blackberry jelly. It was very simple to make because of the high pectin content of the berries.

> 1 gallon blackberries
> 2½ cups sugar
>
> *1 5-quart non-aluminum cooking vessel*
> *Potato masher or pestle*
> *12 clean, dry 5-6 ounce jelly jars with covers*
> *Paraffin*

Pick over the berries, discarding any leaves or stems. Place them in a large colander and run cold water over, then drain well. Take out about 3 cups of berries and put them into the cooking vessel, crushing them with a potato masher or pestle. Add the rest of the berries and set the kettle over a medium flame. Bring to a boil, adjust the heat, and stir with a clean wooden spoon, making sure that the berries do not burn or stick. Cook slowly but thoroughly for 25 to 30 minutes, depending upon how many berries you are cooking. Stir them thoroughly while they are cooking. Remove kettle from stove and cool a bit. Mash the cooked berries and pour them through a coarse strainer into a clean crock. Make a bag of unbleached muslin or linen napkins and pour the strained juice into it, then hang it on a hook that is arranged so that juice drips into a glass jar. (If you are in the country, it's a good idea to cover the jar with a thin cloth to prevent any spiders or other insects from falling into the strained juice.) Leave to drip overnight or until it is finished.

Heat the sugar for about 5 or 10 minutes in 350° oven, leaving the door ajar. Set the jars in a pan of water over a low burner and let them simmer while doing the next step.

Measure out the juice and use 4 cups of it. Put the juice into a wide saucepan and bring to a boil. While it is boiling add the heated sugar and stir to prevent from caking. Cook rapidly for 10 to 15 minutes, then test for jelling point. This is important because juice can cook beyond the stage at which it jells. To test: Skim off any scum that rises on the surface. Insert a spoon into the boiling syrup and hold it above the kettle, tilting the spoon on its side. If the syrup runs to the center of the spoon and gathers into two or three drops and all three fall away together, the juice has reached the right degree to jell. If it falls in one single drop, it needs further cooking. Another test is to drop some syrup onto a cold saucer. If it sets without spreading, it has cooked enough.

Pour into the sterilized jars and fill to ⅛ inch from the top. Set in a draft-free place to cool. When cold, melt enough paraffin and pour over to fill the rest of the space in the jar. When paraffin becomes cold, cover and store in a cool dry closet.

Note: If the berries are bought in city markets and freshness is uncertain, use equal amounts of sugar and juice. The pectin content is higher in fresh-picked berries and less sugar is required.

Spiced Seckel Pears

Seckel pears were one of the earliest ripening pears, deliciously sweet and crisp; they were used principally to make a condiment of spiced pears. The size and firmness and, of course, their flavor as well as their attractive shape and color, made them just right for preserving.

7 pounds firm Seckel pears

2 teaspoons whole cloves

3 pounds brown sugar (not brownulated)

3 cups vinegar

Makes
10 pints or
5 quarts

1 non-aluminum saucepan

10 pint or 5 quart Mason jars

Wash and pare the Seckel pears, leaving them whole with the stem on. In a non-aluminum saucepan place the cloves, brown sugar, and vinegar. Set over a medium burner, bring to a gentle boil, and cook for 5 minutes. Then place the pears in the syrup and simmer them gently until tender when pierced with a sharp, pointed toothpick. Remove from the burner and leave to set overnight. The next morning, remove the pears, strain the syrup into a clean saucepan, heat it to a boil, and boil briskly for 5 minutes. Return the pears to the syrup when the contents come to a gentle boil. Have ready a pan with enough sterilized jars to fill. While both the jars and the pears are boiling, fill the pears into the jars. When full, press the pears gently under the shoulder of the jar and fill the jar to the top with the syrup. Wipe the rim of the jar, place on the jar rubber, if using, and seal. Remove from the hot water and place in a draft-free place until cool. Store in a dry, cool place.

Watermelon-Rind Pickles

During the melon season we enjoyed many afternoons tasting the different kinds of watermelons. Afterward we would carefully select the thickest rinds and prepare them for pickling. We also saved the seeds from the sweetest melons and put them out to dry as our seed for the next season's planting. The varieties we always planted were Jackson, Congo, and Tom Watson. They were very large melons and also very sweet.

1 large watermelon

Makes approximately
3½ quarts

SALT AND ALUM SOLUTION
1 tablespoon salt
1 teaspoon alum
1 gallon cold water

SYRUP
½ ounce Ceylon stick cinnamon
2 pieces dried ginger root
1 piece fresh ginger root, if available
2 blades mace
3 pounds sugar
2 pints cider vinegar
3 slices lemon with the seeds removed

1 5-quart non-aluminum cooking pot
3 1-quart plus 1 1-pint Mason jars, or a
    similar combination

Cut off the green outer skin of the watermelon and discard any pink flesh left inside, because that becomes very tough when pickled. Cut the trimmed pieces of rind into 2-inch strips or 1½-inch squares, and rinse well. Mix the salt and alum together with the gallon of water, stirring until both are dissolved (the alum is what firms the rind). Then put the rind to soak overnight in this solution. In the morning remove the rind from the solution and wash in cold water 2 to 3 times. Drain well.

Meanwhile, prepare the syrup by tying the spices in a piece of clean cheesecloth. Dissolve sugar in vinegar. Add the spices and lemon and set over a medium burner. Bring to a gentle boil and cook for 10 minutes.

Now put the rind pieces in the prepared vinegar and sugar syrup. Place over a medium-high burner. Bring the contents to a gentle boil and cook at a good simmer for 30 minutes. Remove from the burner and let set overnight. Remove the spices. Heat up again the next morning to a gentle boil. When heated thoroughly (15 minutes) have ready sterilized Mason jars in a pan of simmering water. Fill the jars with pieces of rind. Boil up the syrup, then pour it over the pickles, covering them with syrup. Insert a dinner knife into each jar, pressing it against the pickles to release any air bubbles. Gently press the pickles under the shoulder of each jar. This will keep the pieces from floating to the top of the jar. See that the syrup is covering the pickles. Wipe the rim of the jar and seal. Remove from the stove and set the jars in a draft-free place until cold. Store in a dry, cool closet.

Citron Preserves

Citron is a fruit that was generally grown for making into preserves. It had the same color and markings of a watermelon, and the same smell when cut. The flesh was white and the seeds dark gray to brown. The preserves had a much higher, more exotic flavor than watermelon-rind preserves and were not as brittle—they were soft and plump. The preserved pieces were used in cakes, custard-type puddings, candy, and also as ordinary preserves.

Citron preserves have an Old World flavor. They are to watermelon what quince is to pears in flavor. The plants yield an abundance of fruit that keeps well into late fall. One needs to plant only 3 or 4 seeds to get a good supply of citron melons. The seeds are sold by a few seed houses that carry a wide variety of Old World vegetables.

5 pounds citron
2 tablespoons salt
2 teaspoons alum powder
Cold well water or bottled water to cover

Makes about 3½ quarts

SYRUP
3 pounds sugar
3 cups water
3 to 4 slices lemon

sterilized pint jars

Cut the citron in half, remove the seeds, and cut the flesh into rectangular pieces 2½ inches wide and about ½ inch or more thick. Mix the salt, alum, and water and put the pieces to soak in this mixture for 4 to 5 hours. Remove from the salt-alum water and wash the pieces well in two waters, then drain well. While the citron is draining, make a syrup of the sugar and 3 cups water. Heat the water and sugar gently to a boil and cook for 15 minutes. Add in the slices of lemon, the well-drained citron pieces, and cook until a bit transparent and tender. Remove the slices of lemon and put the citron preserves into 10 hot, sterilized pint jars, seal, and set in a draft-free spot until cool. Store in a dry place.

Cucumber Pickles

Pickles, relishes, spiced fruit, jellies, and jams played an important role in the make-up of each meal, especially the meals of fall and winter. The arrival of the hunting season brought a rich variety of game—rabbits, squirrels, birds—and hog killing produced an abundance of fresh pork. There was also the barnyard fowl fattened from fallen grain, nuts, and berries. It all called for a vinegar-flavored accompaniment. Green salads of young and tender leaf lettuce and baby onions were served only in early spring. The spring warmed early in Virginia and the lettuce bolted and went to seed. The rest of the seasons we returned to pickles and relishes.

In midsummer Mother would make a 25-gallon barrel of brine, using water and enough salt to float an egg. (That was a test of the strength of the brine.) The barrel was placed in a cool, shady spot. Every morning while the dew was still on the vines Mother would pick the medium-sized cucumbers with some of the stem left on and drop them into the brine. She repeated that until the vines stopped bearing. The brine was covered with a thick layer of grape leaves from the arbor. In early October she would begin making pickles. This continued late into the fall.

Pickling, as was other canning and preserving, was woven into her everyday work. She would set the pickles to cook after supper and leave to marinate overnight, canning them the next day or perhaps the day after. This would be repeated until the cucumbers were all put up. Then she went on to making her favorite chowchow from the unripened tomatoes that hadn't had time to mature before the frost fell. Of course, there was an earlier preserving of watermelon rind, spiced peaches and Seckel pears, jellies and jams. A company dinner table was studded with a jeweled array of cut-glass dishes, luscious rounds of jade-green cucumber pickles, dark amber, syrupy, glazed, stemmed Seckel pears, pale green squares of transparent watermelon rind pickle, all interspersed with dishes of rich, clear, wine-colored grape and blackberry jellies, adding an exotic flavor to the meal.

Pickles were not made from the kind of cucumbers usually found in the market. Our pickling cucumbers were about 3½ inches in length, rather bumpy, with light and dark green streaks running the length of the cucumber. The garden variety can be found in some markets from early until late fall. To simplify the recipe for making cucumber pickles, I have listed it in five steps.

6 pounds cut-up cucumbers

7 sterilized 1-pint jars with glass tops

Step 1.   BRINE
            1 gallon cold water
            ½ cup salt

Bring the water to a full boil, add salt, stir well, and remove from the burner to cool.

Wash the cucumbers well, drain on a clean, dry towel, and slice into ¾-inch rounds. When all the cucumbers are sliced, drop them into the cold brine and leave to set overnight. Next morning, remove the cucumbers from the brine, wash them in a pan of cold water, and place them on a dry, clean towel.

Step 2.   ALUM WATER
        1 gallon cold water
        ½ tablespoon powdered alum

While the cucumbers are draining, bring a gallon of water to a boil, add alum, stir well, and plunge all the cucumbers into the boiling water. See that all of the pieces are touched with the hot water. Remove from the burner and leave the cucumbers in the alum water for an hour. Remove from the alum water, plunge into cold water, and rinse well. Dip the pieces out and place on a clean towel to drain.

Step 3.   SYRUP
        1 quart cider vinegar
        2 pounds granulated sugar
        1 pound light-brown sugar (not brownulated)
        1 3-inch stick Ceylon cinnamon
        1 2-inch piece fresh ginger root
        3 tablespoons mixed pickling spice

Take a large, good-quality stainless or enamel pan,* put in the vinegar, sugar, and spices tied in a clean piece of cheesecloth. Bring

* We always line our 5-quart cooking pan with clean grape leaves before adding the cucumbers. If you can find unsprayed grape leaves, I recommend your doing it this way.

the mixture to a boil and cook for 15 minutes. Spill in the cucumbers and cook steadily but gently for 45 minutes. Remove from the burner and set in an out-of-the-way spot until the next day.

Step 4. On the next day drain the juice from the pickles and boil it for 15 minutes. Remove the cheesecloth containing the spices and add in the cucumbers. Heat very hot, cooking the cucumbers no more than 3 or 4 minutes.

Step 5. In the meantime, set the clean jars in a pan of water, bring to a boil, and fill with the pickles. Fill with the cucumbers first, then add in the syrup. When the syrup has filled the jar up to the shoulder, take a table knife and insert it into the jar to release any air bubbles. Then take the back of a wooden spoon and lightly press the pieces of pickle under the shoulder of the jar at the neck, then fill the rest of the jar with the syrup. Pressing the fruit under the shoulder will keep it from rising to the top of the jar and pressing against the roof of the cover. Jars for preserving all spiced fruit and pickles should be glass with wire clamps to hold the top in place. Because vinegar corrodes metal, glass or cork tops are the only safe sealers. When the jars are all filled, wipe the rims in case of spillage. Place the rubber ring on each and cover. Put the clamps in place and remove the jars from the water. Set in a draft-free place to cool. When cold, store in a clean, dry place to age.

To Can Green Beans

One of the ways to preserve green beans for winter was to can them. Green beans for canning were ones that had fully developed green pods—not the tender, slender ones for quick boiling and served with melted butter. Beans are a low-acid vegetable requiring long and thorough cooking when canned, and we put them up by the cold-pack method, but then always cook them further (See p. 124). Today, home economists recommend canning under pressure, so follow the directions that come with your pressure cooker in place of the method in step 4. The beans should be free of blemishes or rotten spots, firm and of even length; they should be picked early in the morning while crisp, or purchased when they first come into market.

5 pounds whole green beans   *Makes 10 pints*

*10 sterilized pint jars with lids and screw-on
    bands
1 large kettle or lobster pot for blanching beans
1 canner made up of a large enamel or stainless
    container with cover and wire rack that will
    hold half the jars without touching, so the
    water can flow under and between*

Step 1. To prepare the beans for canning, wash first to remove any dust or trash from the pods. Drain and snip off the ends, leave whole, cover, and keep them cool until ready for canning.

Step 2. To blanch the beans, fill a large kettle with cold water, cover, and bring to a rolling boil, then add the beans a few at a time, so as not to stop the boiling. Add half the beans and boil rapidly for 3 minutes, then dip them out of the boiling water and place them in a pan. Repeat with the rest of the beans. While the second batch is cooking, start the canner to heat.

Step 3. Begin to pack the jars with the blanched green beans. Pack each jar by gathering up carefully enough even-sized beans to fill the pint jar. Put the pods in vertically, up to within ½ inch of the top. While filling, have a saucepan of water heating. When all of the jars have been filled with the beans, add the heated water to within ½ inch of the top. Wipe the mouths of the jars with a clean cloth. Place lids on with sealing composition against the glass rims. Screw on metal bands as tightly as possible. Do not try to tighten them again later, and do not invert the jars. You can tell whether your jar is vacuum-sealed if the top is sucked down tight and makes a hollow sound when tapped; if it is not sealed, the top will bulge out slightly and it has a full, dull sound when tapped.

Step 4. (See introductory note to this recipe on p. 97.) For our cold-pack method: have your canner heating on the burner, filled about one-third with water, steaming but not boiling. Place 5 or 6 of the filled jars on the wire rack (as many as the canner will hold comfortably—see utensils above) and lower slowly into canner. Add enough lukewarm water to cover the jars. Place lid on the canner. Boil for 2½ hours. Be sure to count from the time the water begins to boil (you can hear it boil without lifting the cover). Turn off heat and do not wait for water to cool, but immediately lift out the rack and set jars in a draft-free place without touching until cool. Repeat with remaining jars. When cold, set in a cool, dry closet.

Plum Wine

Wine-making was an integral part of canning and preserving. When berries or small fruits were gathered, an extra pail was picked for wine. In wine-making, as in jelly-making, a few berries or fruit of a different kind were thrown in for added flavor and would become a conversation piece when the wine was served. Ripe fruit of good flavor was used.

8 pounds ripe plums   *Makes about 2½ quarts*
3 pounds sugar
1 small yeast cake (½ ounce), or 1 package
   active dry yeast
A handful of blackberries, grapes, or
   elderberries (optional)

1 non-aluminum cooking pot
1 5-gallon stone crock
2 1-quart bottles plus 1 pint bottle

Wash the plums (and optional additional fruit) and put them into an enamel kettle or a good stainless-steel pot, with enough well water or bottled water to just cover the fruit. Set over medium heat, bring to a gentle boil, and cook gently but steadily for 40 minutes. Remove from the stove and cool. When cold, press the cooked fruit through a strong jelly bag into a stone crock. Measure out 1 gallon of juice and add to it 3 pounds of sugar. Stir and add in the yeast. Tie the jar over with a clean white cloth and leave to ferment for 3 weeks. After 3 weeks of fermenting, pour the wine into sterilized bottles, being careful not to pour any sediment into the final bottles. Discard any sediment. Cork the bottles and leave to age at least 6 months, or as long as you wish.

It is said "never put new wine into old bottles" but we always did and the wine kept very well.

Blackberry Wine

Blackberry wine was made in the same manner except in cooking. Blackberries should be cooked only 25 minutes in well water that is just level with the berries and not over the top.

WHEAT THRESHING

Wheat harvesting came at the peak of summer, usually mid-July. Everyone was very tense the moment the men began cutting the wheat, as the hot weather carried the threat of thunderstorms and rain, which could descend at any moment and put a stop to the threshing.

Our whole county was serviced by one threshing machine that moved with carefully calculated timing from one farm to another. On the day the thresher was scheduled to come to Freetown, all the men were expected to be standing by and ready to begin work as soon as it arrived. By the evening before, all the wheat would have been cut and put into shocks. The thresher would get to us early in the morning, moving slowly down the road, looking like a huge elephant with a giant pipe protruding high into the sky, followed by the operating crew in wagons, with their red and blue handkerchiefs tied loosely at their necks; then came the water wagon loaded with barrels of cold water for the workers.

When the machine started up, the men had to work fast and furiously. The two who worked at the end of the pipe would sometimes be covered with the straw that flew at them wildly as they struggled to make neat stacks. It took a number of men to operate the machine, others to bring the shocks of wheat from the fields, more men to bag the wheat as it came down another chute. It was hot, sweaty work, and the waterboys were kept busy running around with pails of water. By noon the wheat was usually all threshed and the huge threshers would move off to set up at another farm.

Early that morning Mother and some of the neighbors would have gone over to the farmhouse to help with the dinner and the kitchen would be turned upside down. Fortunately, this was the time when the garden was at its peak, yielding forth all of its fruits, so there would be many, many dishes to prepare. The women would set up tables under the shade trees and when dinner was ready one of the cooks would go out and ring a giant dinner bell so that it could be heard all over the countryside. And the men would gather hungrily around the tables that were laden with so many good things:

boiled pork shoulder, braised beef, fried chicken with gravy, baked tenderloin, new cabbage, pork-flavored beans, hot spiced beets, baked tomatoes, potato salad, corn pudding, an assortment of pickles, hot corn batter bread, biscuits, and sliced loaf bread; and for dessert, blackberry cobbler, jelly layer cake, canned peaches, iced tea, lemonade, and buttermilk. After such a dinner, they would stay around and relax a while before moving on to the next farm, where they would continue working until all the wheat in the area had been threshed.

When calm was restored we would assess the yield of our crops. Some of the wheat would be saved for seed and the rest taken to the mill and ground into flour; if there was any surplus it was sold to the miller. We always used the threshed straw to make a summer mattress. First we would stitch together some ticking, leaving an opening for the straw, then we would stuff the mattress to a thickness of about three feet. It was always a delight when we children first slept on one of these newly made straw beds—such a welcome relief from the hot feather tick of winter.

On other hot summer days between wheat harvesting and Revival, we would often enjoy an afternoon of feasting on homemade ice cream or a bowl of crushed peaches. It seemed that there was always something delicious to reward us at the end of any hectic work.

WHEAT-HARVESTING
MIDDAY DINNER

Platters of Sliced Boiled Pork Shoulder
Beef à la Mode
Pan-Fried Chicken with Cream Gravy
Casserole of Sage-Flavored Pork Tenderloin
First Cabbage of the Season with Scallions
Pork-Flavored Green Beans
Spicy Baked Tomatoes
Whipped White Potatoes
Hot Buttered Beets
Corn Pudding
Cucumber Pickles
Pearl Muffins—Biscuits
Butter
Fresh Blackberry Cobbler
Jelly Layer Cake
Iced Tea
Lemonade
Buttermilk

Boiled Pork Shoulder

Smoked pork shoulder was used mainly for seasoning because it was not too fat and had a rich, full flavor—more so than other cuts. But on such occasions as wheat threshing, when there were lots of people to feed, the shoulder was boiled and served sliced with the rind left on. Every bit of it tasted so delicious, and I often think how interesting it is that each cut of pork has a different flavor. I guess that is one reason we never tired of it.

We always prepared and cooked a pork shoulder just the way we did a ham, so follow the recipe on page 138.

For recipe for **Beef à la Mode,** see page 242.

Pan-Fried Chicken with Cream Gravy

The way we fried chicken produced a deliciously crispy outside with just the right amount of moisture inside—never wet at the bone. That raw and very objectionable taste is usually encountered when chicken is fried in deep fat; also, the outside crust is apt to be more tough than crisp. When you pan-fry chicken, put in only enough fat so that it comes halfway up the side of the pieces, because as you add more chicken, the fat in the pan will swell. The fat should be sizzling hot as the chicken goes in and the pieces should be fried briskly until both sides have taken on a good, rich brown. To fry chicken well, you should stay near the stove and give it your full attention, turning each piece perhaps two or three times to get that even color. Mother was an expert at this. If she was cooking a lot of chicken at once, she would brown the breasts first, then stack them up on other pieces that required longer cooking, such as the legs and thighs, after she had turned them over. Because the breast was tender it would finish cooking that way just from the heat of the pan and stay nice and hot.

Our chicken was not only carefully tended, it was also fried in sweet, home-rendered lard, fresh-churned butter, and, in addition, we would put in a slice or two of smoked pork for flavor. When the chicken was all done, Mother would quickly remove it to a warm platter and pour off all but 4 or 5 tablespoons of the fat. Then she would stir in 4 tablespoons of flour, brown it quickly, then add fresh skimmed sweet cream and let it simmer properly. Finally she would taste and add salt and pepper as needed. We used cream a lot in summer because that was the time when calves were weaned and it was plentiful, just as was the green grass for them to graze on.

Casserole of Sage-Flavored Pork Tenderloin

The tenderloin of pork is a small strip of meat from the loin. We used to make sausages with the loin but we would always reserve the tenderloin, cutting it into not-too-small pieces and preserving it. It made a quick and easy dish, something to have on hand for an unexpected occasion. We would simply open a jar and reheat the tender pieces in the oven. If you are serving more than two people, you'll need to get two tenderloins because the pieces are so small.

2 pork tenderloins   *Serves 4 to 6*
½ teaspoon crushed leaf sage
4 tablespoons melted butter
¼ cup flour
⅓ cup cold water
1 small clove garlic
Salt and pepper
1 tablespoon chopped parsley

Preheat oven to 375°. Wipe the pieces of tenderloin off with a clean, damp cloth and rub them all over with the crushed sage. Roll in melted butter, sprinkle lightly with a dusting of flour, and put in a small, oblong casserole with ⅓ cup cold water. Tuck in 3 or 4 slivers of garlic, cover loosely, and bake in a 375° oven for 45 minutes to 1 hour, basting about every 12 to 15 minutes. Salt and pepper the pieces and serve in the casserole garnished with finely chopped parsley.

√New Cabbage with Scallions

The first time we would cook and serve our newly grown garden cabbage was on wheat-threshing day. We would cut up many heads and cook them in a large iron pot with the liquid from the pork shoulder and a small amount of fat for seasoning. Cabbage cooked that way was hearty fare, good sustenance for hard-working men. We children usually had the food that was left over from the midday meal that night for supper and thought it was just great. No other food in the world seemed to have quite the good flavor of what was left over from a wheat-threshing dinner.

1 2-pound head new cabbage   *Serves 4 to 6*
⅓ cup tender green scallion tops, cut into ¼-
   inch slices
2 cups boiling water, or preferably stock from
   boiled pork shoulder
3 tablespoons freshly rendered fat from bacon
   or ham
Salt
Freshly ground black pepper

1 3-quart saucepan

To prepare the cabbage, trim away the outside leaves and cut the head into quarters. Cut away the core, leaving just enough to hold the leaves intact. Place the pieces of cabbage in a bowl of cold water for about 15 minutes or so to wash out any dust or bugs, particularly if it has come straight from the garden. Remove, drain in a colander, then place in a 3-quart saucepan and add the scallion tops to give added flavor and color. Pour the boiling water or stock over and toss the cabbage with two spoons to make sure that each piece is scalded. Add the fat so that it coats the cabbage, then turn the burner low so that the cabbage boils briskly but not rapidly for 25 to 30 minutes—any longer and the cabbage will become too soft and its taste will change. Drain. Toss with salt to taste and a good grating of freshly ground black pepper to heighten the flavor. Serve hot.

For recipe for **Pork-Flavored Green Beans,** see page 124.

Baked Tomatoes

Baked tomatoes added a festive touch to harvesting meals, their sweet and spicy flavor blending well with the mashed potatoes and other summer vegetables. They were thickened with stale bread and seasoned with lots of butter, sugar, and a good sprinkling of ground black pepper.

Serves 4 to 6

2 tablespoons butter
1½ slices trimmed stale bread, cut in 12 pieces
3 cups stewed tomatoes (see page 108)
3½ tablespoons sugar
Freshly ground black pepper

1 1-quart casserole

Preheat oven to 375°. Butter casserole and line the sides with 8 pieces of the bread. Add the tomatoes, sprinkle in the sugar, and dot over with remaining butter. Grind fresh pepper over and then place the remaining 4 pieces of bread on top, dotting each piece with the last of the butter. Bake in a 375° oven for about 35 minutes. Remove and cool a bit before serving.

Stewed Tomatoes

> 1½ quarts ripe tomatoes
> ⅓ cup cold water

Prepare the tomatoes for stewing by dropping them into a pot of boiling water; turn off the burner and leave them for about 3 minutes. Remove the tomatoes to a colander to drain and cool. When cool enough to handle remove the skin, which will peel off very easily when pierced with a knife. Quarter them and remove the seeds, or most of them. When the tomatoes are all peeled and seeded, put them into an enameled, stainless steel, or Pyrex saucepan, add about ⅓ cup cold water, and cook over a medium-brisk burner for 12 to 13 minutes, shaking the pan or stirring with a wooden spoon to see that they aren't sticking. Set aside to cool until needed or can in sterilized jars and seal.

For recipe for **Whipped White Potatoes,** see page 214.

Hot Buttered Beets

These were delicious when the beets were no bigger than a walnut and pulled fresh from the garden.

2 pounds young beets   *Serves 4 to 5*
2 tablespoons melted butter
Salt and pepper

Don't peel the beets and leave on about 1 inch of stem to keep them from bleeding. Place them in a 2-quart saucepan and cover with boiling water. Cook briskly for about 35 minutes. Drain, trim, and peel when cool enough to handle. Serve whole, tossed in melted butter and sprinkled with salt and pepper to taste.

For recipe for **Corn Pudding,** see page 122.

For recipe for **Cucumber Pickles,** see page 94.

For recipe for **Biscuits,** see page 124.

Pearl Muffins

2 tablespoons butter   *Makes 8 muffins*
2 tablespoons sugar
2 eggs, separated
½ cup milk
2 teaspoons Royal Baking Powder
¼ teaspoon salt
1 cup flour
¼ teaspoon vanilla

Cream the butter and sugar together, then add the egg yolks and the milk, stirring until well blended and light. Sift the baking powder, salt, and flour together slowly into the batter and stir until all is incorporated. Beat the egg whites until they form peaks, then fold them into the batter. Add vanilla. Fill buttered muffin tins about two thirds full. Bake in a 350° oven about 15 minutes. Serve hot.

Fresh Blackberry Cobbler

Blackberries were always a favorite with us and fortunately the small berries ripened just about the time the wheat was harvested so that we could have a cobbler for the dinner. The berries grew abundantly along nearby streams and in wet spots in the woods and we would go out early in the morning to pick them, gathering a quart or a gallon in a very short time. Everyone looked forward to a pie or a cobbler during the season. The cobbler was baked in a large, deep baking pan with a delicious crust made from home-rendered lard and baked to a golden brown, with syrupy juice spouting through the pierced top as the berries cooked. It was served warm with the delicious juice from the berries spooned over the top.

PASTRY   *Serves 6 to 8*
2 cups sifted unbleached flour
½ teaspoon salt
½ cup lard
⅓ cup cold water
1 cup crushed cube sugar
¼ cup light cream

FILLING
5 cups blackberries
4 thin slices butter

¾ cup granulated sugar
2 teaspoons cornstarch

8 x 8 x 2-inch baking pan

Sift the flour and the salt into a large mixing bowl. Blend in the lard with a pastry blender or with your fingers. When it is well blended and fine-grained, sprinkle all the water in at once, and draw the dough together quickly, shaping it into a ball. Divide in half and let stand for a few minutes. After it has rested, roll out one piece and line the baking pan. Sprinkle 2 or 3 tablespoons of the crushed sugar over the dough, cover with wax paper, and set it into the refrigerator (or freezer) until you are ready to fill it, along with the other piece of dough. When you are ready to assemble the cobbler, remove the dough from the refrigerator and roll out the top crust. Remove the pastry-lined pan from the refrigerator and fill it with berries, distributing the pieces of butter and sprinkling over the ¾ cup granulated sugar mixed with the cornstarch. Wet the rim of the dough in the pan and place the top pastry over, pressing down all around to seal and trimming away excess. With the handle of a dinner knife, make a decorative edge and then cut a few slits in the center to allow steam to escape. Brush the top with a thick brush of cream and sprinkle on the remaining crushed cube sugar. Place in a preheated 450° oven and when the door is shut, turn down to 425° to bake for 45 minutes. Remove from the oven and set on a rack to cool a bit before serving.

Jelly Layer Cake

A quick and easy way of making a cake for a large number of people is to make it in layers and fill it with a good, tart, homemade jelly, which we did quite often. When we were all working in the fields, one of us—or perhaps it would be Mother—would leave a bit early and go home to stir up a cake for dessert, filling it with one of the tart jellies she had put up.

⅓ cup butter   *Makes 1 9-inch layer cake*
1 cup superfine sugar
2 medium eggs, beaten
2 cups sifted flour
1 cup milk
¼ teaspoon salt
2 teaspoons vanilla extract
3 teaspoons Royal Baking Powder
1 4-ounce jar tart jelly, grape or currant

2 9-inch cake pans

Preheat oven to 375°. In a large mixing bowl, blend the butter until it becomes a bit shiny. Add the sugar and beat until light in texture. Stir in the beaten eggs and blend well. Then begin adding flour, alternating with a little milk, stirring well after each addition and ending with the last of the flour. Add salt and vanilla and finally the baking powder, stirring it in quickly and then spooning the batter immediately into the cake pans, which have been buttered and floured on the bottoms only. (It is better to leave the sides free so that the batter can cling, thus enhancing the rising of the cake.) Place the tins in the center of the oven, preheated to 375°, and bake for 25 to 30 minutes or until the cake begins to shrink away from the sides of the pan. You can also test by picking up the pans and listening to hear if the quiet noises the cake makes while baking have become faint. Remove from the oven and turn the cakes out on wire racks. After they have cooled 10 minutes cover them with a clean cloth until completely cool. Then remove from the racks and cover one with a thin layer of grape or currant jelly. Place the other layer on top. It is also attractive to paint the sides of the cake with a little extra jelly, leaving the top plain or dusting it lightly with powdered sugar.

For recipe for **Iced Tea,** see page 131.

For recipe for **Lemonade,** see page 130.

MAKING ICE CREAM ON A SUMMER AFTERNOON

Ice-cream making was another family affair. Many hands were welcome for turning the crank. To facilitate the making of ice cream it is always wise to make the custard early and set it to chill in the refrigerator.

Vanilla Custard Ice Cream

2 cups milk
½ of a vanilla bean (open a bit)
4 egg yolks, beaten
1 cup sugar
¼ teaspoon salt
1 tablespoon vanilla extract
1 quart heavy cream

Makes about 2 quarts

1 1-gallon freezer
2 5-pound bags ice
5 pounds rock salt
1 cork for freezer top

Pour the milk into a saucepan to scald. Add vanilla bean and have the burner medium high. The milk has reached a scald when tiny beads form around the edge of the milk. Never allow it to boil. Have at hand a bowl containing the beaten yolks with sugar and salt added. Remove vanilla bean and pour the milk slowly into the yolk mixture while stirring constantly. Pour the yolk and milk mixture into a clean saucepan. Set this over a medium-high burner, stirring continuously until the milk begins to heat. Lift the pan up and hold above the burner. Raise the flame a bit and stir until a definite coat covers the spoon, about 3 to 4 minutes. At this point set the pan into a bowl of cold water to halt cooking. Strain the custard into a bowl and cool. When cold, add vanilla and heavy cream. Stir well, cover, and set into the refrigerator to chill. It is good to scald the freezer can, dasher, and cover and set them to chill as well.

Have ice crushed small enough to fit properly between can and bucket. Have the salt and crank all at hand. Stir the custard well. Put dasher in place and pour in custard. Fill three-quarters full. Attach the crank, see that it's in properly, lock, and turn very gently to see if it's on correctly. Fill with ice and salt. First a layer of ice, then a layer of salt, repeating until the bucket is filled to the top. Use 3 parts ice and 1 part salt, always being careful not to get any salt into the cream from the top of the can. Turn the can gently the first few turns, then turn as fast as you can, exchanging with someone else as you tire. The ice will be melting continuously as you turn. This is necessary to freeze the cream. Never let it reach the top of the can because it may get into the cream. Tilt the can on the side with the hole to draw off water. Refill with ice and salt. As the cream begins to freeze it will become harder to turn. Continue to turn until it becomes almost impossible. It takes 25 to 30 minutes. Tilt the bucket to drain out water. Unlock crank and lift it off. Wipe off the top of the cream can as well as the sides to prevent any salt falling in when you remove the cover. Have someone hold the cream can in place while you lift out the dasher. With a long-handled spoon scrape the cream from the dasher, lay the dasher on the platter or hand it to the children who usually are waiting to lick it. Dip the spoon into the cream and bring up the frozen part from the bottom by folding the top in. Do this folding motion three or four times. Smooth over and replace the cover. Place the cork in the opening of the cover and pack it again with the salt and ice as you did before freezing. Cover with a burlap bag or any heavy cloth. Set in the bottom of the refrigerator or a cool place for at least 2 to 3 hours before using.

Peach Ice Cream

Vanilla ice cream was a divine, creamy, crunchy concoction, but peach ice cream drew the most applause.

> 3 cups crushed peaches
> 1½ cups sugar

Select peaches that are soft, yet not overripe, because peaches that are too ripe pass their peak in flavor. While the cream is being turned, begin to prepare the peaches. Peel and cut them in quarters and halve them across. Sprinkle with sugar and crush them with a potato masher. When the cream begins to freeze, open the freezer after wiping it off properly and spoon in the peaches. Stir a bit with a long-handled wooden spoon. Replace the top, reset the crank, and continue to turn the freezer as you would for vanilla ice cream.

Bowl of Crushed Peaches

At least once during the summer when we made a freezer of our good, crunchy, vanilla ice cream, we would save some of our precious peaches and have a bowl of them just crushed along with the ice cream. The peaches were grown in our orchard and it was easy to select sun-ripened sweet peaches. They were peeled, sliced, crushed with a potato masher, and sprinkled over with sugar.

To taste peaches at their peak, they should be sweet, firm, and without a blemish. The Southern peaches seem to have more flavor than the California ones. Sometimes peaches from Australia or South America are found to have quite a good flavor when they first appear in the market.

SUNDAY REVIVAL DINNER

Baked Virginia Ham
Southern Fried Chicken
Braised Leg of Mutton
Sweet Potato Casserole
Corn Pudding
Green Beans with Pork
Platter of Sliced Tomatoes with Special Dressing
Spiced Seckel Pears
Cucumber Pickles
Yeast Rolls
Biscuits
Sweet Potato Pie
Summer Apple Pie
Tyler Pie
Caramel Layer Cake
Lemonade
Iced Tea

This menu is typical of what we would serve at our most important social event of the summer season. It was a time when the garden and field vegetables were at their peak, chickens the perfect size for frying, and it was a time for the first cooked hams of the season. The linen-covered picnic tables would be filled with an array of

*meats cooked to a crispy, deep brown, corn puddings, baked
tomatoes, pork-flavored green beans, sweet and pungent beets,
cakes, pies, and ice cream followed by iced drinks and watermelon
slices, all served free to the visiting guests and relatives home on
vacation.*

REVIVAL WEEK

Anticipation of Revival Week began with the first spring planting.
Revival was like a prize held out during the long, hot summer days
when work stretched from the morning's first light until late evening.

Our Revival Week always began on the second Sunday in August.
Memories of slavery lingered with us still, and Revival was in a way
a kind of Thanksgiving. There was real rejoicing: The fruits of our
hard labor were now our own, we were free to come and go, and to
gather together for this week of reunion and celebration.

At the beginning of August, the first harvest was usually over.
The work horses and stock were driven to the large community pasture to graze peacefully for the rest of the summer. Only the milking
cows and riding horses remained behind. With the field work finished, my father and the other men in the community were able to
spend time getting things in order around the house in preparation
for Revival Week. The first chore was to lay in a supply of wood for
all the extra cooking that would be taking place. Any needed repairs
on the summer kitchen were made, the main room was freshly wall-
papered, the fireplace and chimney whitewashed. Whitewash also
brightened up the outside trim, the fence posts, and even the trunks
of the trees that grew around the house.

Although I didn't think about it at the time, I wonder how my
mother made it each year to Revival Sunday, with so much to do
and without ever varying from the calm and quiet manner that was
her nature. Until the field work, which she loved, was over, she had
no time to begin her own important preparations for Revival Week.
And so, during the week leading up to second Sunday, as well as

doing her regular household chores and caring for her brood of chickens, guinea hens, turkeys, and ducks, and her own vegetable garden, she would cut out and sew new dresses of white muslin for the six of us and our two adopted cousins as well as for herself, usually finishing the last buttonholes and sashes late Saturday night in between the cooking that she would have begun for the next day's noontime dinner at the church.

For my brothers and sisters and me, this was a week full of excitement, with friends and relatives arriving each day from distant cities—Washington, Philadelphia, New York. There were new cousins to play with and we could count on at least one trip into town in the buggy or in the back of the farm wagon to buy staples my mother would be needing, such as vanilla, spices, and sugar. Our own farm and garden yielded all of the flour, butter, lard, meat, vegetables, and fruits that we could use.

My mother never started her cooking until late on the eve of Revival Sunday. By this time she would have everything gathered in and laid out that she would need, and, I guess, a carefully planned schedule laid out in her mind as well. When we were bathed and turned into bed, no pies or cakes had yet been made. But when we came hurrying down on Sunday morning, the long, rectangular dining-room table would be covered with cakes ready to be iced and pie dishes lined with pastry dough to be filled and baked. While we counted them and excitedly discussed our special favorites and how many slices of each we could eat, my mother was out in back feeding her fowl. When she came in she would make us breakfast, standing at the stove with her everyday calm. Then she would help us dress, tie on our ribbons, and send us to sit on the porch until noontime with firm warning to sit quietly so that our new clothes would not get mussed. It would seem a very long morning.

Mother would return to the kitchen to continue her cooking. Because she liked to arrive at the church with the food piping hot, my father would attend the morning service alone and then come back for us as soon as it was over. We would be so excited as we climbed into the surrey. I remember how very special I felt in my new dress which helped me overcome the discomfort of having to wear shoes for the first time since March when school had let out. After we were all squeezed in, my father would load on the carefully packed baskets of food. The savory aroma of fried chicken, so warm and close, always pricked our appetites and long before we reached the church, which was only two miles distant, we would be squirming impatiently, though silently.

The churchyard would be filled with people as we drove up; I felt as though everyone was looking at us. My father would drive straight up to one of the long tables that were stretched out in a line under the huge, shady oak trees alongside the church. My mother would spread out a white linen tablecloth before setting out the baked ham, the half-dozen or more chickens she had fried, a large baking pan of her light, delicate corn pudding, a casserole of sweet potatoes, fresh green beans flavored with crisp bits of pork, and biscuits that had been baked at the last minute and were still warm. The main dishes were surrounded with smaller dishes of pickled watermelon rind, beets and cucumbers and spiced peaches. The dozen or so apple and sweet potato pies she had made were stacked in tiers of three, and the caramel and jelly layer cakes placed next to them. Plates, forks, and white damask napkins and gallon jars of lemonade and iced tea were the last things to be unpacked.

All along the sixty-foot length of tables, neighbors were busy in the same way setting out their own specialties. There were roasts and casseroles, cole slaw and potato salads, lemon meringue, custard, and Tyler pies, chocolate and coconut layer, lemon cream, and pound cakes.

When all the food had been placed on the tables, an unspoken signal would ripple down the line and we would all stand quietly while the minister spoke a grace of thanksgiving. We always liked him, for he knew to keep it short. When the solemn words ended, neighbor would turn to neighbor and warm handshakes, hugs, and affectionate welcomes would be exchanged.

And then at last everyone would come forth and be served, guests and friends first, children last. Second Sunday always seemed to have been a perfect day, with everyone looking their best, eating and chatting. My mother and the other ladies were eager to see that all of the guests were served, and there was always a special plate for a special friend. We usually stood behind our table admiring all the sights. There would be two more days of feasting during the week besides a round of visiting and entertaining in every home in Freetown. The festivities ended for us on Friday, when the visitors stopped by to thank us and say good-bye, promising to return next summer.

For recipe for **Baked Virginia Ham,** see page 32.

For recipe for **Virginia Fried Chicken,** see page 76.

Braised Leg of Mutton

When the miller announced he would butcher a sheep on a Saturday, you understood it would be mutton. It was usually available after the sheep had been sheared. Lambs were never butchered; they were sold off or kept for wool. Mutton, the meat of a sheep three years and older, has a stronger, more exotic flavor than "lamb" and is very delicious when properly prepared.

When buying mutton now, you have to be sure it's from a reliable butcher, and there are few that sell it. Lamb is only a trade name today. It is neither lamb nor is it mutton; it is really a sheep of an age between the two.

1 leg of mutton   *Serves 8 to 10*
½ teaspoon thyme
2 teaspoons salt
2 tablespoons soft butter
1 quart cold water
6 to 8 peppercorns
1 bay leaf

2 small onions
2 to 3 cloves
1 small clove garlic

Take the leg of mutton and trim it close. Saw the small end of the leg bone off as close as possible and, starting at the top end of the leg, pull as much of the skin off as possible or cut it away. Crush the thyme and salt together and mix it with the soft butter. Rub this mixture over the leg of mutton. Leave to set for an hour. Have a heavy oval pot available. Add 1 quart of cold water, the peppercorns, bay leaf, the onions stuck with the 2 or 3 cloves, and the garlic. Set the pot over a medium-high burner and bring to a boil. When boiling, put in the leg of mutton. Cover with a tight-fitting cover and set the pot to cook in a 350° preheated oven for 3 hours, basting every 20 minutes. The long slow cooking will bring out the interesting flavor of the mutton while giving it a rich pale-brown color. When cooked, remove the mutton to a platter and strain the cooking liquid into a saucepan. Set over a burner to heat and to cook down a little if necessary. Pass this heated sauce with the mutton when it is served.

✓ Sweet Potato Casserole

3 pounds sweet potatoes   *Serves 8 to 10*
¾ cup granulated sugar
8 tablespoons (½ cup) butter
½ teaspoon grated nutmeg
1 pint rich milk
3 tablespoons crushed cube sugar

1 3-quart casserole

Place the sweet potatoes (yams are not a good substitute because they are too soft) in a pot of boiling water and cook them until they are barely tender, about 40 minutes. Remove the potatoes from the water and leave them to cool. When they are cold, skin and slice them into ¼-inch pieces and place the slices in layers in a 3-quart casserole. Over each layer sprinkle about 2 tablespoons of granulated sugar and dot it over with 2 tablespoons butter. Continue this process until all the potatoes are used up, stopping only halfway to sprinkle grated nutmeg over the middle layer. Add in just enough milk (approximately a pint) so that it covers everything but the top layer of potatoes. Finally, dot the top layer with butter, add a sprinkling of nutmeg and the crushed cube sugar. Set in an oven preheated to 350° to cook for 45 minutes. The top should be crusty around the edges, a rich brown color, and crunchy when chewed.

✓ Corn Pudding

Corn pudding was one of the great delicacies of summer and the first corn dish of the season. After helping to thin out the corn and weed it, we watched eagerly for the day when Mother served her rich, aromatic, golden-brown corn pudding. It was always served with a sweet potato casserole made from fresh-dug sweet potatoes.

The sauce from both dishes mingled together in the plate combining in a flavor that was memorable. The richness of the dishes reflected the season of the year—a time when there was a plentiful supply of milk, butter, and eggs.

2 cups corn, cut from the cob   *Serves 6 to 8*
⅓ cup sugar
1 teaspoon salt
2 eggs, beaten
2 cups rich milk
3 tablespoons melted butter
½ teaspoon fresh-grated nutmeg

1 1½-quart casserole

Cut the corn from the cob into a mixing bowl by slicing from the top of the ear downward. Don't go too close to the cob—cut only half of the kernel. Scrape the rest off. This gives a better texture to the pudding. Sprinkle in the sugar and salt, stir well, mix the beaten eggs and milk together, and pour the mixture into the corn. Add the melted butter. Mix thoroughly and spoon the mixture into a well-buttered casserole. Sprinkle over with nutmeg. Set the casserole into a pan of hot water and set this into a preheated 350° oven for 35 to 40 minutes or until set. Test by inserting a clean knife into the center of the pudding. If it comes out clean it is done.

Note: An ingenious way we had to retain the freshness of corn was to stand the ears in a tub of water about 2½ inches deep. When the ear is severed from the stalk, its source of moisture is cut off. By standing the corn in a dish of clean water, the cob continues to absorb moisture. Refrigeration, of course, helps, but how many ears will your icebox hold?

Pork-Flavored Green Beans

Serves 4 to 5

½ pound cured smoked pork shoulder or bacon
1 quart cold water
1 quart canned green beans (see page 97)
Salt and pepper

Wash the piece of pork, removing any salt or residue, and make a number of slices in the meat without separating it into pieces. Put the pork into a 2-quart saucepan of cold water. Set on burner and cook slowly for an hour. Then remove the piece of meat, but keep the stock boiling. Open and drain a quart of canned beans, then add to the boiling stock. Cook rather briskly for 25 to 30 minutes. Add salt and black pepper to taste, but be careful because cured meat usually has enough salt to season the pot. The beans are more flavorsome when cooked earlier and reheated for dinner. Serve hot, garnished with thin slices of the boiled pork.

For recipe for **Sliced Tomatoes with Special Seasoning,** see page 85.

For recipe for **Spiced Seckel Pears,** see page 90.

For recipe for **Cucumber Pickles,** see page 94.

For recipe for **Yeast Rolls,** see page 11.

Biscuits

3 cups sifted flour
1 scant teaspoon salt
½ teaspoon baking soda

Makes about 1½ dozen

    4 teaspoons Royal Baking Powder
    ⅔ cup lard
    1 cup plus 2 tablespoons buttermilk
       (If sweet milk is being used, omit the baking
       soda and the 2 tablespoons of milk; sweet
       milk is more liquid than sour and therefore
       these are not needed.)

Take a large bowl, sift into it the measured flour, salt, soda, and baking powder. Add the lard and blend together with a pastry blender or your fingertips until the mixture has the texture of corn-meal. Add the milk all at once by scattering it over the dough. Stir vigorously with a stout wooden spoon. The dough will be very soft in the beginning but will stiffen in 2 or 3 minutes. Continue to stir a few minutes longer. After the dough has stiffened, scrape from sides of bowl into a ball and spoon onto a lightly floured surface for rolling. Dust over lightly with about a tablespoon of flour as the dough will be a bit sticky. Flatten the dough out gently with your hands into a thick, round cake, and knead for a minute by folding the outer edge of the dough into the center of the circle, giving a light knead as you fold the sides in overlapping each other. Turn the folded side face down and dust lightly if needed, being careful not to use too much flour and causing the dough to become too stiff. Dust the rolling pin and the rolling surface well. Roll the dough out evenly to a ½-inch thickness or a bit less. Pierce the surface of the dough with a table fork. (It was said piercing the dough released the air while baking.) Dust the biscuit cutter in flour first; this will prevent the dough sticking to the cutter and ruining the shape of the biscuit. Dust the cutter as often as needed. An added feature to your light, tender biscuits will be their straight sides. This can be achieved by not wiggling the cutter. Press the cutter into the dough and lift up with a sharp quickness without a wiggle. Cut the biscuits very close together to avoid having big pieces of dough left in between each biscuit. Trying to piece together and rerolling leftover dough will change the texture of the biscuits.

Place the biscuits ½ inch or more apart on a heavy cookie sheet or baking pan, preferably one with a bright surface. The biscuits brown more beautifully on a bright, shining pan than on a dull one, and a thick bottom helps to keep them from browning too much on the bottom. Set to bake in a preheated 450° oven for 13 minutes. Remove from the oven and let them rest for 3 to 4 minutes. Serve hot.

Sweet Potato Pie

DOUGH

Makes 2 10-inch or 3 7-inch pies

3 cups plus 2 tablespoons sifted flour
1 cup chilled, home-rendered sweet lard
1 scant teaspoon salt
½ cup cold water

FILLING
2 cups mashed and sieved sweet potatoes
1 cup sugar
½ teaspoon cinnamon
½ teaspoon fresh-grated nutmeg
½ teaspoon salt
3 small or medium eggs, separated
2 teaspoons vanilla extract
⅔ cup butter, melted over hot water
1⅔ cups milk, at room temperature

2 10-inch or 3 7-inch pie pans

In a mixing bowl blend well together with a pastry blender the 3 cups of flour, lard, and salt. When well blended, add cold water and mix together by hand. This is a very short dough and the water has to be incorporated in by hand. After blending the water in, shape the dough into a ball. Sprinkle the dough over with 2 tablespoons flour to make it easier to handle. Divide the dough into pieces for the number of pies to be made. Leave to rest for 10 to 15 minutes. It is best to roll the dough out after resting. It is easier to handle while soft. After rolling the dough out, place it in the pie pans, trim, cover, and set in the refrigerator or freezer until needed. Remove and fill while chilled.

In a mixing bowl combine the sieved sweet potatoes, sugar, spices, salt, beaten yolks, vanilla, and melted butter. Mix thoroughly. Add in the milk and stir well. Beat the whites of eggs to the frothy stage and stir them into the batter. Pour the batter into the pastry-lined pie pans. Bake in a 350° oven for 40 to 45 minutes.

Summer Apple Pie

The apple pie that I remember was made from fresh homemade applesauce, sweetened to taste and flavored generously with freshly grated nutmeg. The seasoned applesauce was spooned into a pastry-lined pie plate and covered with a top crust. When baked and completely cooled, the pies were removed from each pan and stacked one upon the other. When the pie was sliced you were served a wedge with three layers.

PASTRY   *Makes 3, 7 or 8-inch pies*
3 cups sifted unbleached flour
½ teaspoon salt
1 cup lard, chilled
½ cup ice water

APPLESAUCE
1 cup sugar
1 teaspoon freshly grated nutmeg
3 pounds apples, peeled, sliced, and cooked as on
    p. 238

3 8-inch pie plates

Mix the pastry dough according to directions on page 41. Divide
it into pieces to fit the bottom of each of the three pie plates and a
little less for the top crust. This is a soft dough and it is best to roll
it out and place it in the pie plates, then chill until needed. The top
pie crusts can be rolled out, placed on wax paper, and set to chill as
well. It is important to remove the top crust from the refrigerator
ahead of time in order for it to warm up. If not, it will become
brittle and break in half when unfolding. The bottom crust should
remain chilled until it is filled.

Add sugar and nutmeg to applesauce. Mix well and spoon 1½
cups into each pastry-lined pie plate. Moisten the rim of the pie shell
and place on the top crust; seal the two by pressing the rims together. Make 5 or 6 vents in the top of the crust—the more vents
there are in a two-crust pie the crispier the crust will be. Bake about
45 minutes in an oven preheated to 425°. When done, remove from
oven and set on a rack to cool.

For recipe for **Tyler Pie,** see page 136.

Caramel Layer Cake

5 tablespoons butter   *Makes 1 9-inch layer cake*
1 cup sugar
¼ teaspoon salt

2 medium-sized eggs, at room temperature
2 cups sifted flour
⅔ cup milk, at room temperature
2 teaspoons vanilla extract
1 teaspoon freshly squeezed lemon juice
4 teaspoons Royal Baking Powder

2 9-inch cake pans

Put the butter in a large mixing bowl and with a wooden spoon work the butter until it becomes shiny, about 4 minutes. Add sugar and salt. Blend together until the mixture becomes quite light. Add in an egg and stir one way, clockwise. Add second egg and stir until all the grains of sugar disappear. Sift in ½ cup of flour, stir in, but not too thoroughly. Add ¼ cup of milk and stir vigorously. Alternate the rest of the flour and milk, ending with flour. Mix the flour and milk in a way that keeps the batter from separating. Pour the milk into the flour before it is completely mixed in. This will keep the batter completely smooth. Before sifting in the last bit of flour, add flavoring. Then add the baking powder to the last batch of flour, sift in together, and stir well. Spoon the batter into the buttered and floured cake pans. Set in the center of the middle shelf of a pre-heated 375° oven. Bake 25 minutes without opening the oven. Test to see if done by noticing if cake has shrunk from the sides of the pan. Also, listen for any quiet noises from the cake. If there are none, that's a sign it is done. Remove from oven, run a spatula around sides of pan, and turn out right away on a wire rack. Cool for 5 minutes, then cover with a clean towel until ready to ice it.

CARAMEL ICING
1 cup heavy cream
2¼ packed cups light-brown sugar
   (not brownulated)
2 tablespoons butter
2 teaspoons vanilla extract

Heat the cream until hot in a saucepan but do not allow it to boil. Add in the sugar and mix well. Boil gently on a medium-high burner and cook to soft stage—that is, when it forms a soft mass when a little is dropped into a cup of cold water. You should be able to pick it up even though it is soft. Remove from burner when this stage is reached. Set the saucepan in a bowl of cold water, add butter and vanilla, stirring continuously until the mixture becomes thick enough to spread. Remove pan from the bowl of cold water. Place one layer of cake on serving platter. Spread about one third of the icing over the top. Place second layer on iced layer and pour remaining icing in the center of the top layer and spread it over top and down the sides. (If the icing becomes too thick to spread, add a tablespoon or two of cream to soften.)

Set the cake in a dry tin. It is better not to store cake in the refrigerator. It becomes heavy and loses its light, fluffy quality.

Lemonade

The festivity of Revival, of almost any picnic, or of a hot afternoon at home was heightened when a stone crock of tangy lemonade was brought out with a big, free-form piece of ice and thin slices of lemon floating on it. It would be ladled out in tall glasses and the cool drink always fitted the occasion, whether it was chatting with friends under the shady oaks at Revival or relaxing at home after a hot morning of work in the fields. Often we would stir up a quick cake to serve with lemonade. Warm cake was a favorite in Freetown.

2 cups sugar	*Makes 10 glasses*
½ gallon well water*	
1½ cups freshly squeezed lemon juice	
Ice	

* If you don't have a well, use bottled spring water.

1 lemon, sliced into thin slices
Fresh mint (optional)

Dissolve the sugar in the well water. Add the lemon juice, a solid piece of ice, and lemon slices. This can be put into a stone crock or a glass ice bucket and decorated with mint, if desired.

Iced Tea

Iced tea was a very popular drink at picnics and Revival meetings. It was served only on special occasions with the addition of crushed mint that grew abundantly in the spring. The aroma of freshly crushed mint heightened the festivity of any occasion.

We used only the whole leaves of a good-quality orange pekoe or a blend of green tea. The tea was properly steeped and poured over a piece of ice made from pure spring or well water. I have found tea bags give an off-flavor to the tea and the dust contents of the bag is a poor substitute for good, whole leaves. Perhaps the lack of authentic flavor has caused iced tea to become just another fruit punch.

2 ounces orange pekoe *Makes 12 glasses*
3 quarts boiling water
Ice
Mint or lemon slices

1 1-gallon crock, scalded with hot water

Place the leaves in the scalded crock and pour the boiling water over them. Let steep only 7 to 8 minutes. Then strain the hot tea through a stainless-steel strainer over a 1-quart piece of ice. This will prevent the tea from becoming cloudy before being served. Allow each person to sweeten his own tea to taste. Serve with a sprig of mint or lemon slices.

A COOL-EVENING SUPPER

✓Summer Vegetable Soup

Store Soda Crackers

✓Ham Biscuits

Cucumber Pickles

Tyler Pie

Coffee

On a cool evening, we might have a summer vegetable soup containing all the fresh vegetables grown in our garden served for a change with delicious, crispy Uneeda biscuits from the Lahore store or, for company, ham biscuits made from leftover ham, cucumber pickles, and for dessert a golden-brown Tyler pie.

✓Summer Vegetable Soup

Summer was a more appropriate time to have vegetable soup than winter. Only in the late spring and summer, when the miller killed a cow on orders from the neighborhood, did we have a meal with beef. Also, it was during this period that we made vegetable soup.

The meat was of high quality, producing a strong and well-flavored stock. Even though the meat was of a good flavor, we always added chicken parts, a piece of pork, and especially the feet of the chicken, which first were scalded, scaled, and despurred. No one ever threw the chicken feet away; they gave body to the soup as

well as some flavor. This goes for pork as well. Added to the meat
and bones were the fresh-picked garden vegetables: butter beans,
string beans, fresh corn cut from the cob, tomatoes, peeled and
seeded, wild and cultivated herbs, and snips of leaves from celery.
Root vegetables and onions were omitted because of the hot weather
and the quick spoilage of the onion in the soup.

One has to search hard to find beef with a satisfactory flavor. To
obtain the most from that which is offered in the market today, the
meat should be simmered very slowly in just enough water to cover
and cooked for 5 to 6 hours.

3 pounds shank with the bone   *Serves 6 to 8*
6 peppercorns
1 pound of the bony part of the fowl
2 chicken feet, if possible (prepared as above)
1 onion, stuck with 3 or 4 cloves (optional)
½ pound sliced smoked pork, or salt pork with
     streak of lean
A few sprigs of parsley
Celery stalks with a few of the leaves
1 cup butter beans
1 cup cut green beans
1 cup shredded cabbage
1½ cups fresh corn, cut from the cob
2 cups peeled, seeded, and finely chopped
     tomatoes
Salt

1 8-quart pot

Wipe the beef with a damp cloth and brown well by searing it on a
hot skillet. Place all of the beef into an 8-quart pot. Add the peppercorns and enough cold water to just cover the meat. Set over a
burner and bring to a simmer but never allow the contents to boil.
Cook at a quiet bubble for 5 to 6 hours. Halfway through the cook-

ing, add in the chicken pieces, optional onion, pork, and the parsley and celery. When the meat becomes tender, remove it from the pot. Strain the broth and return to the kettle. Heat to simmer. Add the vegetables and cook for 1 hour, simmering. Salt to taste. Remove all the fat from the soup and serve with crusty yeast bread. Sometimes the meat from the piece of shank was cut up and sprinkled with black pepper, or served the next day with a spicy horseradish sauce. The rest of the bony pieces were divided among the pets with nothing going to waste.

HORSERADISH SAUCE
4 tablespoons butter
3 tablespoons flour
1½ cups hot milk
4 tablespoons grated horseradish
½ teaspoon salt

Take a quart saucepan, put in the butter, and melt it over a low burner. Add the flour and cook slowly, stirring all the while, until the mixture becomes well blended. Then cook until it just begins to turn slightly brown around the edges of the pan. Pour in the hot milk. Stir well and continue to cook very slowly for 25 to 30 minutes. Strain and add in grated horseradish and salt. Mix well and serve hot with the boiled beef.

Soda Crackers

It was a great novelty to have Uneeda biscuits or soda crackers once in a while with soup or cheese. They were always fresh-tasting, crisp, and delicious with soup, especially the summer vegetable soup. They came in bulk and one could buy as many as one wished.

Ham Biscuits

The women of Freetown were amazing because they participated in the work of the fields and barnyard and yet would step right out of the field work when an unexpected friend or traveler turned up. They would make a quick fire in the wood cookstove, and in a few minutes emerge from the kitchen with a pot of hot coffee, a plate of biscuits—flannel-soft, a thin slice of ham inserted in each—a bowl of home-canned peaches, and perhaps some sugar cookies. Often the biscuits were made with chipped pieces of ham—the remains after the ham was sliced—and that is what this recipe calls for. Ham biscuits were usually served at ball games and suppers, and always at Sunday Revival.

Follow the recipe on page 124 and add 1 cup finely minced ham just after you have added the milk.

For recipe for **Cucumber Pickles,** see page 94.

Tyler Pie

There are many recipes for Tyler pie or pudding. This recipe has been around Lahore one hundred years and I suspect it is pretty close to the original, since Tyler was born in Orange County. The women of Freetown each praised the perfection of their Tyler pies. It was served throughout the year along with seasonal pies.

Pastry for 2 8-inch pie pans   *Makes 2 8-inch pies*

FILLING
4 eggs
2 cups sugar
1 teaspoon flour
½ teaspoon salt
1 cup (½ pound) slightly melted butter
1 teaspoon vanilla
1 teaspoon lemon extract
2 cups milk

2 8-inch pie pans

Prepare the dough according to directions on page 217 and line pie pans. Chill until ready to fill.

Beat the eggs well, then add sugar mixed with flour and salt. Continue to mix well and add in the butter, vanilla, and lemon extract; stir well and pour in the milk. After one final stirring pour the mixture into the two pastry-lined pans. Bake in an oven preheated to 350° until set and golden brown, about 30 to 35 minutes.

A COOL-EVENING SUPPER

Warm, Sliced, Boiled Virginia Ham

Lima Beans in Cream

Smothered New Cabbage

Hot Spiced Beets

Watermelon-Rind Pickles

Biscuits

Butter

√Fresh Peach Cobbler with Nutmeg Sauce

Coffee

There was always a cool evening brought on by a heavy thunderstorm and this would be a night for a boiled ham. The meat with the skin on was often served warm and invariably thought to taste more delicious with new boiled vegetables and the first peach cobbler of the summer.

Boiled Virginia Ham

It is said that pigs were brought to Virginia from England during the 1600's, and the meat developed soon became one of the most popular meats in the cookery of the region. Perhaps it is the acorns, peach pits, peanuts, corn, and maybe some truffles found in the oak forest of Virginia, plus the smoked hickory cure taught by the Virginian Indians, that has given the Virginia ham the delicious flavor for which it is famous.

A Virginia ham is one "raised and cured in Virginia." The best are local-cured. The next best is Gwaltney. For those not familiar with cooking Virginia ham: It must first be washed and scrubbed with a stiff brush to remove the moldy covering that usually coats the ham. Preferably soak overnight in water to cover, then discard the soaking water. Cook in enough cold water to fully cover. If the ham is being cooked without soaking, the water should be changed midway through cooking. Discard first cooking water and start over with fresh hot water to cover. Bring the ham to a near simmer, then adjust the burner to hold the cooking to what we always called a mull—just a quiet bubble. Never let boil; as the meat cooks through the heat will have to be adjusted to keep it below the boil. Keep the water above the ham by adding hot water as it is cooked away. Cook for at least 6 hours, at which time the bone begins to protrude at the top of the ham. Test the ham for tenderness by piercing with an ice pick or a skewer. If the ham seems too hard, leave to cool in the cooking liquid for 2 hours.

Remove to a rack to drain and set for 15 minutes. Slice with a sharp, wide-bladed knife. It is easier to slice with the skin on while still warm. Trim some of the skin off the slices and some fat—but not all; ham fat is flavorsome and goes well with the lean in a boiled dinner.

For recipe for **Lima Beans in Cream,** see page 217.

Smothered New Cabbage

Serves 6

1 medium head (about 2 pounds) new cabbage
3 tablespoons fat, rendered from smoked meat
   or bacon
1 tablespoon vinegar
Salt and black pepper

Trim the outside leaves away from the cabbage, then cut it in half. Slice it into shreds ¼ inch thick. Heat an iron or other heavy skillet hot and add the fresh fat. Add in the cabbage and let it sear without browning. When well seared, 3 to 4 minutes, sprinkle in vinegar. Cover the pan with a close-fitting lid and let the cabbage cook for 20 minutes, stirring occasionally. Season with salt and black pepper to taste. Serve hot.

Hot Spiced Beets

4 medium beets   *Serves 6*
2 teaspoons butter
1 tablespoon sugar
¼ teaspoon black pepper
½ teaspoon salt
1 tablespoon vinegar
1 tablespoon chopped fresh chervil

Place the beets in a saucepan of boiling water (enough water to cover the beets by about 3 inches) and cook gently for 1 hour and 15 minutes until tender. Drain away the liquid, slip the skin from the hot beets, and slice them into ⅛-inch pieces. Dot with butter, sprinkle over the sugar, black pepper, salt, and vinegar. Keep warm until ready to serve. Finally, sprinkle over with chopped chervil.

For recipe for **Watermelon-Rind Pickles,** see page 91.

For recipe for **Biscuits,** see page 124.

Fresh Peach Cobbler with Nutmeg Sauce

Traditionally in Freetown, we always made a lattice top, rather than a regular top crust for peach cobbler. It was the great hot fruit dessert of the summer season that everyone looked forward to enjoying and I give it here in three parts.

PIE CRUST   *Serves 6 to 8*
2 cups all-purpose unbleached flour
¼ teaspoon salt
½ cup lard, chilled
⅓ cup cold water

1 8 x 8 x 2-inch baking pan

Take a mixing bowl, sift in flour and salt. Add chilled lard, and blend with a pastry blender or your fingertips until the mixture becomes the texture of heavy cornmeal. Sprinkle over the cold water and mix together lightly until the dough sticks together. Shape into a ball and leave it in the bowl to rest for at least 15 minutes. Divide the dough in half. Roll out one piece of the dough and line baking pan that has been greased lightly with lard. After pressing the pastry gently over the bottom, sides, and corners, trim the overlapping dough from edges of pan. Cover with wax paper and set into refrigerator until needed. Roll out the second piece of dough and cut it into 8 strips. Place the strips between wax paper and place them in refrigerator as well.

FILLING
7 to 8 large peaches, washed and drained
1 cup sugar
4 tablespoons (¼ cup) butter

Peel the peaches and slice each into 6 or 7 pieces. When all the peaches are sliced, remove the pastry and strips from the refrigerator. Sprinkle 2 tablespoons of sugar over the bottom of pastry in pan and fill in with the sliced peaches; sprinkle the rest of the sugar over the peaches. Scatter thin slices of butter, 6 to 8 pieces, over the sugar. Moisten the rim of the pastry and place the strips of dough, weaving them in by placing one across and one lengthwise until they are used up. Press down along the rim and trim surplus pastry hanging over edges. Decorate rim by pressing marks on pastry with handle of a dinner knife.

Set the cobbler into the center of a preheated 450° oven, close the door, and turn the oven down to 425°. Bake for 45 minutes. Remove from oven and let cool for 15 to 20 minutes before serving with a nutmeg sauce.

NUTMEG SAUCE
⅔ cup sugar
¼ teaspoon fresh-grated nutmeg
2 teaspoons cornstarch
Pinch of salt
1 cup boiling water
1 3-inch piece of orange peel, dried or fresh
3 tablespoons brandy

Place the sugar, nutmeg, cornstarch, and salt in a quart saucepan, stir well, and pour in the cup of boiling water, stirring as you pour. Add in orange peel and set over a medium burner to boil gently for 10 minutes. Set aside until ready to serve. Reheat without boiling and add in brandy. Serve warm with peach cobbler (omitting the orange peel).

Fall

Unlike other seasons of the year, the coming of fall was looked upon with mixed feelings. When the leaves began to fall, all the visitors were gone, and the whistle from the train passing through Orange gave a long, lonesome, shrill sound as it rolled through without stopping to let off any passengers.

But our spirits always lifted when my father would announce at the breakfast table on a Sunday morning in late September that he was bringing the stock home that day from the community pasture where they had grazed lazily all summer. As soon as my father and my older brother came in sight of the house we would rush out to greet them, admiring how much the calves had grown and how fat and sleek all of the animals were. After patting and stroking them, they were herded into their winter lots and left to get used to being back home.

Our thoughts turned to the opening of school in mid-October and to the harvesting of vegetable root crops, like sweet potatoes, peanuts, the cutting of field corn. After school started, we would rush home, change our clothes, and help gather in the potatoes and do other daily chores.

Once the corn was all cut and stacked in shocks, a group of high-school students who loved my mother would come on the first moonlit night and help us with the corn shucking. They thought it great fun, boys and girls with their favorite friends. After the shucking they would return to the house and be given a festive meal that my mother had had in preparation all afternoon: one of fried chicken, baked ham, roasted, newly dug sweet potatoes, baked tomatoes, green beans, cake, and apple pie—the apple pie being the favorite. The young people ate heartily and left late, thanking my mother and promising to come back the next fall. The next morning the corn field was dotted over with mounds of yellow corn, ready to be picked up and hauled to the corn crib.

Before we fully realized it, we were deep into fall and the other activities related to it, such as Race Day, hunting season, and rehearsing for the Annual Community Concert of Winter.

BREAKFAST BEFORE LEAVING
FOR RACE DAY

**Sour-Milk Griddle Cakes with Warm Blueberry Sauce
and Maple Syrup**

Sausage Patties

Biscuits

Pear Preserves

Damson Plum Preserves

Coffee

RACE DAY

The annual horse race at Mrs. DuPont Scott's estate, Montpelier, is held traditionally on the first Saturday in November and is open to the whole county. For 40 years this has been the main event of the autumn season, and one of the few occasions during the year when farmers, tradespeople, estate owners, and workers mingle together —the men urging and cheering on the horses, placing bets among themselves, and enjoying occasional sips of bourbon, the women busy selling raffle tickets and home-baked foods to raise money for local charities, and enjoying the chance to visit and exchange views and family news.

We would start the day with a good, hearty breakfast of griddle cakes, sausages, hot bread, preserves, jam, and lots of hot coffee to brace us for the brisk November weather.

Sour-Milk Griddle Cakes

1½ cups sifted flour   *Serves 6 to 8*
½ cup whole-wheat flour
½ teaspoon salt
½ teaspoon baking soda
2 teaspoons Royal Baking Powder
1 egg, beaten
1 tablespoon melted butter
2 cups sour milk or buttermilk

Sift flour, salt, soda, and baking powder into a mixing bowl. Add beaten egg and melted butter. Mix well by stirring. Add milk and stir well. Pour on sizzling-hot greased griddle. When the cakes become quite puffed and show tiny bubbles, turn and cook a few minutes more. Serve with stewed blueberries and maple syrup. The combination of blueberries and maple syrup is the tastiest one could imagine.

BLUEBERRY SAUCE
2 cups blueberries, fresh or frozen
⅓ cup sugar
⅓ cup water

Place the berries, sugar, and water into a quart saucepan. Set the pan over a medium flame and bring to a boil. Turn the flame down, leaving the berries at a quiet, rather gentle boil for 3 to 4 minutes. Turn the heat off until the pancakes are ready to serve. Then reheat the berries so they will be hot (do not allow them to boil) and spoon them onto the pancakes. Pour on the maple syrup and it's simply divine.

For recipe for **Sausage Patties,** see page 206.

For recipe for **Biscuits,** see page 124.

For recipe for **Pear Preserves,** see page 40.

For recipe for **Damson Plum Preserves,** see page 157.

RACE DAY PICNIC

A Thermos of Hot Virginia Country-Style Beef Consommé

Cold Roast Pheasant

Salad of Lentils and Scallions

Ham Biscuits

White Pound Cake

Ginger Cookies

Stayman Winesap Apples

Dessert Grapes

Kieffer Pears

Thermos of Hot Coffee

Beautiful Montpelier, nestling in the Shenandoah Valley, surrounded by an oak forest, was the most perfect spot to have a great fall picnic lunch. Everyone would be dressed in the latest fashions to attend the races, even the handsome guest horses wearing the colorful silks of their stables. There was always excitement in the fresh November air and the good, hot, beef consommé seemed to build an appetite for all the good things to follow. There would be a cold roast of aged pheasant, a salad of lentils, fresh-picked scallions from the garden, and ham biscuits. And for dessert, thin slices of white pound cake, tangy ginger cookies, a basket of delicious Winesap apples, sweet dessert grapes, and juicy Kieffer pears, with a thermos of good, hot, black coffee.

Virginia Country-Style Beef Consommé

4 pounds bottom round beef   *Makes about 2 quarts*
1 knuckle and shinbone
3 quarts water
2 chicken backs plus necks
1 large onion stuck with 4 cloves
2 carrots, sliced
1 large leek, top removed
1 bunch celery
1 tomato, peeled, seeded, and finely chopped
4 peppercorns
1 bouquet parsley and bay leaf
¼ teaspoon thyme, fresh or dry
1 tablespoon salt

Preparing a good consommé today requires careful cooking of the ingredients. Meat hasn't the same flavor of years gone by. The best ingredients should go into a pot that you are going to cook in for 6 hours.

Place the beef and bones in a pot containing 3 quarts of cold water. Cover and bring to a slow simmer without ever letting the pot come to a boil. A gray scum will rise on the surface as it begins to heat up. This you skim off and discard. Continue to skim until it is no more. At this point add the chicken and vegetables, peppercorns, and herbs. About halfway through add salt. Cover loosely and barely simmer for 6 hours. Remove from burner, strain, and leave to cool. When cold, skim off all fat. This consommé can be served clear or used as the base for other soups, onion soup in particular.

After 2 hours of cooking, the celery may be removed and reserved for later. When the consommé has finished cooking, the meat may be removed and served later for supper with the celery, heated in horseradish sauce (see page 134).

Cold Roast Pheasant

While many city dwellers may seem to think pheasant is only served under glass, for country folk it was a way of life. In the fall, while harvesting the corn, we would come upon a variety of game feasting on fallen grains of corn. We always carried the rifle, hoping to return to the house at night with a bagful. We usually did come home with game of some species. Pheasant is pretty special game, whether caught in the wild or raised in captivity; the flavor remains the same when properly aged. As great as pheasant tastes, it has less flavor than chicken if it is dressed and cooked without aging. If purchased at a game farm or shot in the wild, it is best to let the pheasant hang in a cold place in the feather or let your butcher hold it for you. He will dress it for you as well. When buying pheasant be sure it is fully matured for the best flavor. Some growers try to dress off their birds at 14 weeks, but this is too young. It is simply a way of their saving feed at the expense of flavor. Buy your pheasant from reliable sources.

1 pheasant (allow 1 pheasant for 2 persons)   *Serves 2*
1 teaspoon salt
½ teaspoon pepper
¼ teaspoon thyme
½ cup (1 stick) plus 2 tablespoons butter
Watercress for garnish

Carefully wash and pat dry the outside of the pheasant. Remove the lungs and entrails from the inside cavity and wipe it well with a damp cloth. Do not wash out the cavity, as it will take away some of the special flavor that is characteristic of game birds. Mix together the salt, pepper, and thyme. If the thyme is fresh, cut it fine; if dry, crush it against the salt with a spoon. Sprinkle the cavity with half this mixture and add ½ stick of butter. Rub the outside with 1 to 2 tablespoons soft butter and the rest of the seasoning.

Roast in a covered casserole or roasting pan in the middle of a

425° oven. Allow 1½ hours for cooking. After 15 minutes lower the heat to 350°. Melt the remaining ½ stick of butter, and after reducing the heat, baste every quarter hour with a tablespoon of melted butter. Twenty minutes before the pheasant is done, you may find it convenient to transfer the bird to another casserole to finish cooking so that you can make the sauce, which is easily done. Add 3 tablespoons hot water to the juices in the first casserole and stir well to loosen any particles stuck to the bottom. Strain and reheat just before serving. Remove the pheasant from the oven and place it on a hot serving dish with a garnish of watercress. Or, if you are planning to serve it cold, pour the juices over, and chill in a covered bowl overnight.

Lentil and Scallion Salad

A salad of brown lentils is the most perfect accompaniment to cold roast pheasant. The piquant flavor of lentils and onion against the cold pheasant, marinated in its own juices, is a great experience in picnicking.

½ pound smoked pork or streak of lean (not bacon)   *Serves 6*
1 pound lentils
4 scallions
4 tablespoons olive oil
2 tablespoons wine vinegar
1 teaspoon salt
¼ teaspoon freshly ground black pepper
¼ teaspoon dry Coleman's Mustard

Put the pork up to cook with 4 cups water and simmer for 1½ hours. Remove pork and skim off any fat. Rinse the lentils and drain, then add them to the broth the pork was cooked in. Cook the lentils for about 25 minutes, or until just tender, then drain them and leave them to cool. Slice the white section of the scallions very thin and add them to the lentils. When cold, sprinkle in the dressing made by shaking the oil, vinegar, and seasonings in a screw-topped jar until well mixed. Gently stir the dressing through and leave the lentil salad to marinate for a few hours before serving.

For recipe for **Ham Biscuits,** see page 135.

White Pound Cake

½ pound butter
2⅓ cups superfine sugar
3 cups sifted flour
½ cup milk
¼ teaspoon salt
2 teaspoons almond extract
⅔ cup (about 4 to 5) egg whites

1 10-inch tube pan

Place the butter in a mixing bowl and work it with a wooden spoon until it becomes shiny, about 5 minutes. Add in the sugar and blend until the mixture becomes light and the sugar granules almost disappear. After the mixture becomes well blended, begin to stir clockwise in a circular motion. Add a little of the flour and some of the milk, stirring well after each addition, until both are used up, beginning and ending with flour. Add salt and almond extract. Beat the egg whites until they form soft peaks but are not dry. Fold into the batter, then spoon the batter into the tube pan. Set into a preheated

300° oven. Place on the middle shelf and bake at 300° for 40 minutes, then turn up to 325° for 15 minutes more. Remove from oven
and run a knife around the sides of the pan. Turn out upon a wire
rack, then turn cake face up. Leave to cool. After 15 minutes of
cooling, cover to prevent drying out. When cold, store in a clean,
dry tin.

Ginger Cookies

2 cups sifted all-purpose flour
1 teaspoon Royal Baking Powder
¼ teaspoon baking soda
¼ teaspoon salt
1 teaspoon cinnamon
2 teaspoons powdered ginger
½ teaspoon powdered cloves
4 ounces (1 stick) butter
1⅔ firmly packed cups dark-brown sugar
1 egg, beaten
½ cup Barbados or sorghum molasses

*Makes 3 dozen
or more cookies*

Place the flour in the sifter and add in the leavenings, salt, and
spices. Sift this onto a sheet of wax paper and set aside until
needed. Place the butter in a mixing bowl and work with a wooden
spoon until the butter becomes shiny. Add in the sugar and blend
well. Add in beaten egg, continuing to stir. Add the flour mixture
gradually, mixing well. Add the molasses, stir, and spoon the dough
onto a shallow dish. Cover with wax paper and set in the refrigerator
overnight, or set into freezer compartment until dough is stiff
enough to roll, about 20 minutes.

Remove dough from freezer, cut off a portion, and set the rest
back into the refrigerator. Lightly dust a rolling surface with flour
and roll the dough away from you, shifting the dough to see that

it doesn't stick. Roll out to a thickness of ⅛ inch. Press out with a cookie cutter of your favorite design. Pick each cookie up with a thin pancake turner and place it on a buttered cookie sheet. Bake at 375° for 10 to 12 minutes.

Remove from oven and leave to rest on cookie sheet to cool for 3 to 4 minutes; otherwise, cookies will be too soft to handle. Lift from sheet and place them on a wire rack to cool. Store in a clean, dry, well-covered tin.

Apples

An apple orchard was a basic part of every homestead. It supplied all of the fruit used. The orchard was also a kind of nursery for baby calves when weaned from the mother cow, and a haven for birds, especially bluebirds and robins. The little bluebird always made its nest only in the hollow of an apple tree.

Apples were used in more ways than any other fruit. In early summer, before they were ripe enough to eat, they were best used for making applesauce and, because of their tart flavor, they made the best apple pie. On the hottest days of summer they were peeled, sliced, and dried on the roof of the porch to put away for the winter when we would use them to make apple puffs and pies. They were on the breakfast table every morning during the summer and fall in the form of fried apples. Later in the season there was the making of apple butter. Frankly, I didn't like that very much; I can still smell the cinnamon cooking in it.

Fall was the season to pick apples. On a crisp, clear day we had to stay home from school and help with the picking. Although we liked gathering apples, we hated to miss school. There were countless varieties: early, late, winter, crab apple, and the ones used only for making cider. When they were all picked and culled over, the bulk of the crop was heaped into a cone shape on the ground, covered over with straw and leaves, and then a thick layer of earth. These apples were left stored this way until all the apples in the bin in the kitchen were used up. Then the kiln was opened in February and we had apples until they became sappy and not good to eat. At that point, we turned to canned ones.

During the winter we consumed bushels of apples. After supper, when all the evening work was finished, we would settle down to study and would bring in a basket of apples to munch on. Student friends would join us to help clarify a subject someone didn't quite understand, and we would be up until past midnight studying, singing, reciting poetry, and devouring apples, pickles, and anything else edible.

Although we had many different kinds of apples, there are only a few names that I remember: Early Transparent, Sweeting, Grimes Golden, Ben Davis, Pippin, and the longest, best-keeping, and most delicious—Stayman Winesap. These trees were grown from seed and not grafted. Many are still in the area and continue to bear.

There are a few nursery houses that carry some of the old varieties. One house is Spring Hill Nurseries of Tipp City, Ohio 45366. There is also a system of planting that produces fruit in a shorter time by planting the roots in with stones. It is called the White System. Information can be obtained through Organic Gardening and Farming at Emmaus, Pennsylvania 18049.

If you have a spot of land, do plant a few apple trees, particularly if there are children around to enjoy them. We are still enjoying the apples from trees our parents planted 45 years ago.

Dessert Grapes

The grape arbor was a fixture in every homestead. Near the kitchen door, it gave off a fragrance that filled the back porch and it was a favorite home for the jaybird to build its nest. The grapes were deliciously sweet with a thin, tender skin and a dark plum to black color. They were known as table or dessert grapes. The bunches were not so tightly compact as today's grapes. They were enjoyed while they were ripening. Surplus grapes were stored in an outside shed in sawdust, and that way they lasted down to Thanksgiving.

Dessert grapes can be found in some of the old nurseries, such as Stark Brothers of Louisiana, Missouri, and Kelsey Brothers Nursery of Hillside, New Jersey. Some names of the grapes were Cao, a red grape that ripened around September 20; Golden Muscat, ripening from October 15 to 20; and Fredonia, a black grape.

Making Wine and Persimmon Beer

Wine-making was part of canning and preserving and we would always set aside blackberries and elderberries for that purpose. In the spring we would make a dandelion wine, whereas in the fall there was an abundance of persimmons, which we valued for a kind of beer we would make with them. We would gather the persimmons only after a heavy frost because that was said to sweeten them. We would pick over all that we'd gathered, trim off their caps, and then stir them into a medium-soft batter made from the bran of white cornmeal mixed with spring water. After it was all well mixed, we would spoon the batter into a large bread pan and bake it in the oven. After it had baked and cooled, the cake was placed in a stone crock or a wooden keg with twice as much spring water, then covered and left to ferment until Grandfather decided it was ready for drinking—usually in late winter.

Damson Preserves

The damson tree was one of the most popular in the orchard; more fuss was made over the tree than the preserves. It was a prolific bearer of hundreds of small plums, the shape of birds' eggs, of intense navy-blue with a purple tinge. Damson preserves are the first that I really was aware of, mostly because of the attention bestowed on the tree. They have a tangy and distinctive flavor, especially when preserved with their pits intact, and are particularly good with all kinds of meat. If you watch carefully, you'll find damsons still available in the market for a short period in late September. Get them when they first appear, while they are new and high in pectin count, and preserve them quickly.

3 pounds sound, blemish-free plums

2½ pounds sugar

*Makes 6
5-ounce jars*

1 5-quart enamel preserving kettle
6 5-ounce sterilized jars with covers

Damsons should be processed as soon as they are brought in because any delay will cause the fruit to dry out and lose its tangy flavor. Prepare the plums by first washing them off, draining them carefully, and sticking each plum a few times with a stout needle. Place the damsons into the preserving kettle, sprinkle over with the sugar, and leave overnight. In the morning set the kettle over a medium flame, bring to a simmer, and continue until the plums are tender and the syrup has become thick. (Note: Do not overcook the preserves. Cook only until the fruit is tender and syrup is a clear wine plum color. If the syrup turns brown, it is overcooked.) Remove the preserves from the burner and leave to rest overnight. The next morning heat the preserves until just hot and pour them into the sterilized jars, filling the jars to ¼ inch from the top. Then pour on melted paraffin. When the paraffin becomes set and cold, screw on the tops and place in a cool, dry place.

EMANCIPATION DAY DINNER

**Guinea Fowl in Casserole Garnished
with Watercress**

Steamed Wild Rice

Green Bean Salad with Sliced Tomatoes

Grape Jelly

Parker House Rolls

Butter

**Purple Plum Tart or Stewed Quince
and Special Cookies**

Coffee

---

*We usually served a spring-hatched guinea during the fall with the
last green beans of the season and a delicious plum tart or newly
ripened, fresh, stewed quince.*

Guinea Fowl in Casserole

Guineas were an integral part of every barnyard in Freetown. They were cultivated because of their watchdog quality; they always made a big fuss whenever any stranger appeared. The guinea fowl has its origin in West Africa and their African link was passed on from generation to generation by African-Americans. They were eaten only on rare occasions and had to be shot, as they lived in trees and roamed the countryside. They were treated like any game birds.

1 guinea fowl   *Serves 4*
½ cup (1 stick) soft butter
¼ teaspoon thyme, fresh or dry
Fresh-ground pepper to taste
1 small onion, sliced
1 slice smoked pork shoulder or bacon
½ cup cold water
Salt
Watercress

The flesh of guinea fowl is a bit more dry than game birds and the best way to cook them is to split them down the back. Paint the bird over with soft butter, then sprinkle it with ¼ teaspoon fresh or dried thyme and a light sprinkling of fresh-ground black pepper. Place the fowl in a flat casserole, slice a small onion over the contents of the pan, and add a slice of smoked pork. Add ½ cup of cold water and cover with a close lid. Place in the center of a preheated 350° oven. Cook for at least 1 hour and 45 minutes to 2 hours. Baste every 20 minutes, being careful not to let the pan dry out. When cooked, place on a platter and strain the pan juices over the fowl in the dish. Sprinkle with salt to taste and garnish with watercress.

Steamed Wild Rice

Wild rice grew along the streams that ran through the fields. We never bothered to gather it for cooking, but watched the turkeys enjoy it as they ran their beaks up the cane and pulled off the rice. That's probably why Mother usually received premium price for her turkeys when they were sold. Since then, I have become interested in wild rice and various ideas about how to cook it.

1 cup wild rice   *Serves 4*
Pinch of thyme (wild or cultivated)
1½ cups cold water, or broth (see below)
½ teaspoon salt
¼ teaspoon black pepper
1 tablespoon fat, from chicken, pheasant, or
     turkey while cooking, or butter

Use an enamel-coated iron casserole or a heavy-bottomed saucepan. Put the rice in, and run cold water in to fill the pot so that the chaff and light trash floats to the top. Some grains of rice will rise, too, but save them. Run the water out and see that the water is pretty well drained. Add thyme, crushed between your fingers. Set over a medium-high burner, bring the rice to a quick boil with 1½ cups of cold water, then turn the burner very low to just steam or to the lowest simmer. (One can also make ahead a broth of neck and gizzard of turkey or pheasant [not the liver], and use this broth in place of the water or added with water. But if these parts are not available, just use plain water.) Cook this way undisturbed for an hour, at which time add salt, pepper, and fat from the game, chicken, or turkey that is cooking in the oven. If you have no fat, season with butter. Continue cooking for another ½ hour or longer. If the rice seems too dry, sprinkle over it ¼ cup water and continue to cook until all the water is absorbed. Fluff the rice near the end. It can be cooked ahead, seasoned, and warmed beforehand by setting the casserole, covered, into the oven at 350° until hot.

Green Bean Salad with Sliced Tomatoes

Green bean salad is lovely to look at, brittle, and a delightful taste treat.

1 pound green beans
Salt

Serves 4 to 5

VINAIGRETTE DRESSING
¼ cup vinegar
½ cup olive oil
¼ teaspoon salt
⅛ teaspoon fresh-ground black pepper
2 teaspoons grated onion

GARNISH
Lettuce, tomato, 1 tablespoon chervil

Select a pound of beans that are slender and of the same length and size. Snip off the ends, wash, and drop them into a 3-quart pot of rapidly boiling water over the highest heat. Let the beans boil furiously for 12 minutes, uncovered, skimming off any scum that arises. Add salt while boiling, 2 teaspoons to ½ gallon of water. Drain and plunge the beans into ice water for 2 minutes. Remove the beans from the water and lay them on a clean, odorless towel to dry off. Make a vinaigrette dressing by combining above ingredients with grated onion. Gather the beans into a bundle and place them in a deep, oblong dish. Pour the dressing over them and leave the beans to marinate for ½ hour. Then place them in a loose bundle on a bed of lettuce garnished with sliced tomatoes and a bit of dressing dribbled over. Sprinkle a tablespoon of chopped chervil over it.

Grape Jelly

Among the flurry of fall activities was the hunt for wild grapes. Fox grapes, as they were called, revealed their presence by giving off a strong aroma of grape that permeated the woods and along the streams where they grew. The aroma was especially strong at twilight. We knew from the aroma that they were ready for gathering.

These wild grapes were excellent for jelly-making. Their flavor was sharp, and the jelly made a perfect accompaniment to fresh pork and game. Mother always used it to fill a simple butter cake, which we called jelly layer cake.

Grape jelly is one of the easiest to make, its one fault being the development of rocklike crystals that form in the jelly if the proper steps are not taken! The juice should set overnight and when it is poured off, be careful to leave behind the residue that settles at the bottom. Of course, the jelly is more successful if the fruit is processed as soon as it is picked or as soon as it comes into the market, while the pectin is high and the fruit is not overripe. If possible, it is good to add in some green grapes. All you will need to make the jelly is a good-quality enamel kettle or stainless-steel one of about 5 gallons, a wooden pestle, a large colander, 12 sterilized ½-pint jars, and a box of paraffin.

Wash a quantity of grapes in 2 gallons of cold water and pick the grapes from the stems. Discard all blemished ones. Put a few of the grapes in the kettle and mash with a wooden pestle. Add in a cup of bottled well water. Add more grapes and crush until all are used up. Set on a medium burner to start cooking. Cook gently for 25 to 30 minutes. Remove from the burner and pour the grapes into a colander set over a bowl. Press the juice through with the pestle. Discard the pulp and pour the juice into a gallon glass jar. Measure out 3 cups of juice at a time. For best results only cook in batches of 3 cups at a time. Add an equal amount of sugar that has been heated hot in the oven for 10 minutes. Set to cook on a brisk burner until the juice remains firm when dropped on a cold saucer, or try the spoon test: After cooking for 15 minutes insert a spoon into the boiling jelly. Lift the spoon above the kettle, holding it sideways. If the juice drops off by running into the center of the spoon, forming two drops, and the whole mass falls away in a sheet, it is ready to pour into the jars, filling each ¼ inch from the top. When cool, melt some paraffin and pour ⅛ of an inch thick into the jar. Leave to cool. When cold, screw tops on, label, and store.

Parker House Rolls

The cooks of Freetown loved making yeast bread. Rolls were particularly good for sopping up sauces or gravies from the braised rabbits, quail, and guinea fowl we ate in the fall. We made rolls in a variety of shapes, and the Parker House rolls always reminded me of a folded envelope as we flipped the dough over.

Makes 1½ to 2 dozen

1 cake (½ ounce) yeast or 1 package dry active
   yeast
¼ cup lukewarm water
1 tablespoon plus 1 teaspoon sugar
2 tablespoons butter plus extra for dough
2 tablespoons lard
1 teaspoon salt
2 cups milk
4 cups sifted flour

Dissolve the yeast in ¼ cup lukewarm water with 1 teaspoon sugar. Place the remaining sugar, 2 tablespoons butter, lard, and salt in a bowl. Heat the milk to a scald and pour into the bowl containing the butter mixture. Stir until all is dissolved. When lukewarm, add flour and stir well. When halfway mixed add in the dissolved yeast. Mix well, knead the dough for about 5 minutes, place in a draft-free place of approximately 80°, cover with a towel, and set to rise until it is double in bulk. Push the dough down gently and spoon onto a flour-dusted surface and roll out a little less than ½ an inch thick. Cut with a round biscuit cutter. Butter the surface of each circle of dough. Fold in half and as they are finished place side by side almost touching in a baking pan. This should be done very quickly; the yeast dough will be rising all the while. Preheat the oven to 425°. When rolls have risen to almost double their size and are light to the touch, set them into the oven, turn oven down to 375°, and bake for 20 minutes.

Plums

Plums of all kinds were looked upon as being very special, perhaps because of their deep pastel colors, their different shapes, textures, and sweet flavor. The bright-red round variety were the first to ripen, and were used in preserving and wine-making. Damsons were always made into preserves (see page 157). The pale-green ones called greengages were stewed. And the dark-purple ones were used for pies, tarts, and fruit compotes. Everyone had plum trees in their orchards and new plants were constantly seeded, and the seedlings were passed around from neighbor to neighbor.

Purple Plum Tart

FILLING
1½ pounds purple plums
⅔ cup sugar

PASTRY
1 lightly filled cup plus 2 tablespoons unsifted
   unbleached flour
¼ cup sugar
½ cup (1 stick) butter
¼ teaspoon salt
Grated rind of ½ medium-sized lemon

1 9-inch tart pan, or add shallow spring-bottom cake pan

Wash and drain plums, cut in halves, and discard pits. Place halves in a single layer skin side down in a flat casserole or ovenproof Corning Ware dish. Sprinkle over with ⅔ cup sugar. Set into a preheated 425° oven for about 15 minutes. This is to extract most of the juice. Remove from oven and set aside.

Place 1 cup of the flour, sugar, butter, salt, and lemon rind in a mixing bowl. Blend all together with fingertips and when well blended, knead the dough by hand continuously for 15 minutes. This is the key to obtaining good results from this butter-rich dough. Sift in 1 tablespoon of flour during kneading and a second tablespoon near the end of kneading. This is a very soft dough. Spoon it into an ungreased tart pan or spring-bottom cake pan. Lightly press as you push the dough evenly over surface of pan and around sides, making a rim of ½ to ¾ inch high and about ¼ inch thick.

Place the cooked plums skin side down on the pastry, reserving the juice. Arrange them to look attractive and set into moderate oven preheated to 350° for 20 to 30 minutes. The crust should be light brown in color. Remove from oven, let cool. Set the juice that was extracted from the plums on the burner and reduce to a syrupy consistency, watching not to let it burn. Spoon this over the plums. This should give a beautiful glaze. If you like, the tart can be garnished with a ring of whipped cream but it just as delicious without.

Note: Purple plums are usually plentiful when in season but do not hold very long. They deteriorate rapidly by drying out and losing their tart flavor. Therefore, get your supply early in the season. I chose plum tart over other fall fruits because I feel plums are the most fitting fruit for this butter-rich pastry. It is an easy fruit to find in city markets, but at home we used to make this tart also with regular pie dough. This particular pastry has been worked out after many trials, adjusting the quantities, the amount of kneading, the oven temperature. Butter-rich doughs tend to dry out with the slightest overcooking; it is imperative that a strict watch be kept during the baking.

For recipe for **Stewed Quince,** see page 234.

For recipe for **Special Butter Cookies,** see page 15.

FALL BREAKFAST

Oatmeal with Cream

Smothered Rabbit

Fried Tomatoes

Corn Muffins—Biscuits

Wild Blackberry Jelly

Butter

Coffee—Hot Cocoa

Visitors would arrive for the hunting season a day early to test their skills, and we always had a particularly good breakfast, like this one, the first morning.

Oatmeal with Cream

Hot oatmeal was our standard cereal beginning in the fall through the late spring. After putting up the coffee, oatmeal was next on the stove. We would boil it up and then set it on the back of the stove to heat through. It was served along with the rest of the breakfast and a pitcher of heavy cream. My uncle always ate buttered bread with his oatmeal. It was a great dish for a cold morning when we had to face the winds blowing off the Blue Ridge Mountains on our way to school.

Smothered Rabbit

2 rabbits, cut into 6 pieces each   *Serves 6*
1 cup flour seasoned with ½ teaspoon black
     pepper, ¼ teaspoon thyme, and 1 teaspoon
     salt
½ cup (1 stick) butter
2 slices bacon, chopped
1 medium-sized onion or 4 to 5 shallots, finely
     cut

Roll the pieces of rabbit in the seasoned flour and let them set for 20 minutes. Heat a large skillet and cook the butter until it foams, then add the bacon pieces. When they become a bit browned, remove them with a slotted spoon and put in the pieces of rabbit, except the four front quarter pieces (they can be used later in a soup or stew). Brown on both sides, sprinkle over the browned pieces with defatted bacon, onion or shallot, and ¼ cup water. Cover and set into oven at 300°, or leave to cook on burner slowly for 45 minutes. Serve hot as you would serve fried chicken.

Note: You can buy domestic rabbit frozen, cut-up, and ready to cook in many supermarkets, and in some city neighborhoods you can find whole rabbits in the fur.

Fried Tomatoes

½ cup flour   *Serves 4 to 5*
½ cup unseasoned bread crumbs
½ teaspoon salt
¼ teaspoon pepper
5 medium-sized tomatoes of good shape
2 tablespoons fresh bacon fat, or butter
½ cup soft brown sugar

Sift together the flour, bread crumbs, salt, and pepper. Slice off the top or stem end of tomatoes to get a flat slice. Cut ¼-inch slices and press each one into the flour mixture, coating both sides. Place the floured slices on a sheet of wax paper for a few minutes before cooking. Heat a skillet; when it is hot put in the bacon fat or butter, tilting the skillet to distribute it around the pan. When the butter is foaming or the bacon fat is smoking, put in the tomato slices and cook on a medium-high burner to obtain a good, brown crust. Cook for 4 minutes on each side, turn the tomatoes over when browned, and sprinkle the browned top with ½ teaspoon brown sugar. Remove from the skillet and serve hot.

For recipe for **Corn Muffins,** see page 81.

For recipe for **Biscuits,** see page 124.

For recipe for **Wild Blackberry Jelly,** see page 89.

Hot Cocoa

A pan of hot cocoa was usually resting on the back of the stove during the chilly season. It was a second beverage for grownups and a hot drink for the children who wanted it. Cocoa, like coffee, filled the kitchen with its exotic aroma. The brand we used was Baker's Breakfast Cocoa. When you're buying cocoa today, look for a brand that has no additives or sweetening.

4 cups milk   *Serves 4 to 5*
4 tablespoons cocoa
4 tablespoons sugar
Pinch of salt
1 3-inch stick of Ceylon cinnamon
Gratings from 1 fresh nutmeg

Place the milk in the top of a double boiler, cover, and set it over the burner to heat. While the milk is heating, in a small bowl mix together the cocoa, sugar, and salt. When the milk is quite hot pour about a cup of it into the bowl containing the cocoa mixture. Mix well and then pour this cocoa mixture into the milk in the double boiler. Stir until well mixed. Add the stick of cinnamon and a good grating of nutmeg. Cook the cocoa for another 15 minutes. Turn off the heat and let the cocoa rest over the hot water until it is ready to be served.

HUNTING SEASON DINNER

Quail in Casserole

Purée of Green Black-Eyed Peas

Steamed Lamb's-Quarters or Broccoli Rabb or Kale

Crispy Biscuits

Butter

Green Tomato Preserves

Hazelnut Pudding with Custard Sauce or

Warm Poached Kieffer Pears

Coffee

HUNTING SEASON

Hunting season was as much a part of harvesting as was hog butchering, turkey picking, gathering of nuts, berries, persimmons, and apples. Rabbit, quail, squirrel, plover, snipe, woodcock, and wild turkey lived in the woods and surrounding fields feeding upon hickory nuts, hazelnuts, persimmons, corn, and other cereal grains and frequently feeding with barnyard flocks. Hunting was not a sport of killing but a way of adding variety to the food supply, making our meals more interesting and delicious. Game had the distinction of holding for a long time; after it was drawn, most game with fur and feathers left on was left to hang in the meat house and used as needed. Plover, snipe, and woodcock were not around much, but when we did have a rare bird we would often add it to quail or other more plentiful game. The juices would mingle together as they cooked, resulting in an unusually delicious flavor.

We enjoyed game throughout the fall and winter and especially at Christmas, adding variety to the holiday menu.

Quail in Casserole

Quail are small birds and we usually added other game near the end of cooking, sometimes a squab chicken.

STUFFING   *Serves 4 to 5*
5 slices stale bread with the crusts removed
⅓ cup milk
Livers from quail and squab, finely chopped
¼ cup melted butter
¼ teaspoon sage
Salt and pepper

6 quail
1 squab chicken
1 cup plus 3 tablespoons butter
3 slices bacon
Salt and pepper
¼ teaspoon thyme
½ pound mushrooms, sliced
½ pound seedless white grapes

Prepare the stuffing by soaking the slices of bread; put them in a dish and pour milk over, letting them stand a minute. Take the soaked slices two at a time and squeeze tightly by hand. When all the milk is squeezed out, loosen the bread by pulling it apart with your fingertips. Mash the liver with a fork and mix well with the bread. Pour the melted butter over the bread mixture, sprinkle in sage, salt, and black pepper.

Prepare quail by wiping inside and outside with a damp cloth. (Washing game will take away some of the flavor peculiar to game.) Stuff the birds with the dressing and sew the opening up with a needle and thread (the stitches will be removed before serving). Rub them over with soft butter.

Wash the squab chicken under cold water and wipe dry. Have at hand a heavy iron or enamel casserole heating with 3 tablespoons of the butter. Heat up a second heavy skillet and add ½ cup of butter. When it is foaming, put in the squab chicken. Sear well on both sides and then place the squab in the center of the casserole, skin side down, spreading the bacon around it. Quickly sear the quail in the same pan, then set the quail on top of the squab chicken. Sprinkle the birds lightly with salt, thyme, and fresh-ground pepper. Place on each bird a thin pat of butter. Set the pan into a preheated 350° oven for 45 minutes. Near the end of the cooking, sauté the sliced mushrooms in about 3 tablespoons butter for 4 to 5 minutes over a high flame, stirring. When the birds are done, take a heated platter and place the squab chicken in the center skin side up, arrange the quail around, and sprinkle the dish with the sautéed mushrooms. Squeeze ¼ cup of juice from the grapes and pour it into the pan the quail was cooked in. Loosen all particles on bottom and sides, blend well, and season to taste. Then pour this hot sauce around the quail. Serve hot.

Purée of Green Black-Eyed Peas

Black-eyed peas were popular in the late summer and fall. They were not planted in the garden but were planted by farmers as a green manure crop. Before the sowing of wheat, when in full foliage, they were chopped into the soil. A week before, everyone was welcome to gather the green pods before the crop was chopped under. Everyone responded and we enjoyed fresh black-eyed peas for a short period. The black-eyed pea is truly an African bean, first introduced into our area by Thomas Jefferson, via France. France was always an exponent of agriculture and found this legume high in nitrogen and other soil-building qualities.

Preparation of Leafy Greens
(Kale, Rape, Mustard, Lamb's-Quarters, Wild Watercress, Purslane, Broccoli Rabb or Turnip-Top Leaves, Beet Tops)

Boiled leafy greens are not fully appreciated because most people don't know how to prepare them. First of all, they need not be greasy. The most delicious cooked greens we made were cooked with pork, except for spinach, and we usually served them with a white sauce. Some varieties of leafy greens we would gather and cook every day, mostly because we knew instinctively that they were of nutritional value—an instinct that comes from our African heritage, I'm sure. Even though nutrition was our major concern, we always prepared them in a manner that made them taste very delicious.

Smoked pork shoulder or side of cured bacon—middling, as it was called—was used. The meat was usually boiled until done, then the greens were added to the boiling stock. Dry-cured pork does not give off that much fat—just enough to give the greens a shiny glaze. Most important is the flavoring of the stock. And the greens should be fresh and crisp, with any heavy stems broken off, leaving only the leaves. (Stalks can be tied into a bundle and used for stock.) After the leaves have been well washed and drained, plunge them into the boiling stock; you should have about 3 pounds greens to 1 quart stock. Immediately stir the greens to see that they all get blanched by the boiling stock. Press the greens down lightly in the stock and cook them fast but gently for no more than 15 to 20 minutes. Cook uncovered, which prevents them from turning brown. Remove them from the burner and let them sit in the broth, partly covered now. Gently reheat and then drain them when ready to serve.

Broccoli rabb can be put into a wide-bottomed pan, using only the water clinging to the greens after washing. Cover with a tight lid and cook for 15 minutes. Heat ¼ cup olive oil and ½ clove garlic. Drain the broccoli rabb and pour the hot oil over it, discarding the garlic. Stir by lifting up the leaves to let the oil run through. Beet tops can be treated in the same way.

Note: Greens purchased in the city markets today are sometimes old and can be very bitter. It is a good practice to blanch them first in a large pot of boiling water for 3 minutes before cooking them in the stock.

Kale is most tender when it has not yet reached the curly stage. Mustard, broccoli rabb, rape, watercress, and beet tops are all best when young and tender as well. Lamb's-quarters, purslane, and wild cress can be gathered in the wild in the proper stage.

Crispy Biscuits

There were many variations in the making of biscuits to suit the particular occasion; for instance, for ring mold of chicken (see page 28) and casserole of quail, thin, crisp biscuits were more appropriate than the light, soft ones we served at breakfast and other meals.

2 cups sifted unbleached flour
¼ teaspoon salt
½ teaspoon baking soda
2 teaspoons Royal Baking Powder
5 tablespoons butter
⅔ cup sour milk or buttermilk

*Makes about
16 biscuits*

Sift the flour, salt, soda, and baking powder into a mixing bowl. Cut the butter into small pieces and add to the flour mixture. Blend this mixture with your fingertips or a pastry blender until it becomes grainy and heavy as cornmeal. Sprinkle in the milk and mix with a stout wooden spoon. Shape the dough into a ball and place it upon a lightly floured surface. Knead for a minute or two, giving quick, rolling punches into the dough. Then roll out to ¼ inch thickness, pierce the dough over with a dinner fork, and cut it out with a 2-inch cutter. Place the biscuits about an inch apart on a heavy cookie sheet or baking pan. Set into a preheated 475° oven for 10 to 12 minutes until nicely browned. Remove from the oven, let rest a minute or two, and serve hot.

Green Tomato Preserves

The season for preserving garden products was brought to a close with two of the most exotic fruits: green tomatoes and a vine fruit known as citron. Our vines were filled with many tomatoes that had no chance of ripening in the cool weather of late September and had to be gathered early to avoid being bitten by the first early frost. Some of the green tomatoes were wrapped in tissue paper and stored in a cool, dark place on the dirt floor, then proudly presented at hog killing or Christmas; others were made into chowchow pickles. But best of all, we liked green tomato preserves. Their taste against a hot biscuit is very much like that of mild honey. These were the preserves we liked to present when company came.

3 pounds uniform size (2 to 2½ inches in   *Makes 8*
    diameter) round green tomatoes   *½ pint jars*
3 pounds sugar
2 slices lemon, ¼ inch thick

1 5-quart preserving kettle
8 ½-pint glass jars, sterilized
Paraffin

Select firm green tomatoes, wash, and wipe them dry. Examine them carefully to see that no worms are lodged in the stem end. Cut a slice off the stem end making a flat, smooth surface, and slice away any blemishes from the tomato. Then prick it in four or five places with a needle. Place the tomatoes in the preserving kettle, sprinkle with sugar, and leave to set overnight. By morning the sugar will have dissolved and there will be enough liquid in which to cook them. Add the slices of lemon and set the kettle on a medium burner; when the contents begin to simmer, lower the burner to keep the kettle at a steady, slow simmer for one hour. (By that time the tomatoes will have become quite transparent.) Remove from burner and leave to rest overnight. In the morning set the kettle over a hot burner until it just begins to boil. Then take a slotted spoon and lift the tomatoes one by one out of the pot and place them in a bowl. Pour the syrup through a clean, odorless piece of cheesecloth or a stainless strainer, catching all of the loose seed that fell out in the cooking. (There will be plenty more seed in the tomato.) Reheat the preserves to a simmer and pour them into the dry and sterilized jars. Pour over ⅛ inch of melted paraffin. When the paraffin becomes cold, screw on tops, label, and place in a cool, dry place.

Note: I could sense a great feeling of satisfaction on my mother's face when she had reached the point of placing the labels on the jars after the completion of each batch of preserves and jellies.

√Hazelnut Pudding with Custard Sauce

⅓ cup granulated sugar   *Serves 4 to 5*
1 cup milk
2 tablespoons butter
1 tablespoon flour
3 egg yolks, beaten
¼ teaspoon salt
1½ cups ground hazelnuts
2 teaspoons vanilla
2 tablespoons rum
6 egg whites, beaten
Confectioner's sugar

Add the sugar to the milk and scald over a hot flame. Melt the butter in a saucepan, stir in the flour, and pour in the scalded milk. Cook for a few minutes, stirring continuously over a medium-low flame. Remove from burner and add beaten egg yolks, stir, and add salt, hazelnuts, vanilla, and rum. Mix well again and fold the egg whites, beaten until almost stiff, into the hazelnut batter. Spoon into a buttered pudding mold or soufflé dish, about 1½ quarts, filling it three quarters of the way, and set the dish into a pan of hot water. Place in a preheated oven at 350° for 25 minutes. Sprinkle over with confectioner's sugar and serve hot with custard sauce.

CUSTARD SAUCE
¼ cup sugar
3 egg yolks, beaten
2 cups milk
1 teaspoon vanilla extract, or rum

Combine the sugar and the egg yolks. Scald milk and pour into beaten yolk mixture while continuing to stir. Strain the mixture into a saucepan and hold it above the burner while stirring until a good coat develops when a clean spoon is inserted into the custard. The minute the custard reaches that point set the pan into a bowl of ice-cold water. Flavor the custard and pour into the serving container without stirring so as not to break up the custard.

Warm Poached Kieffer Pears

The favorite fall fruit was stewed Kieffer pears. Kieffer was a late pear for winter use. It was highly aromatic and juicy when ripe. Some of the earlier ripening ones were stewed. When cooked they would fill the house with an aroma that warmed the atmosphere on a late fall afternoon.

Kieffers have more body than Bartletts and more lasting flavor. They can be found in the market in early October, and trees are sold by Spring Hill Nurseries, Tipp City, Ohio 45366. The trees last for 50 years and more.

4 cups cold water
2½ cups sugar
½ vanilla bean
6 ripe Kieffer pears

Place the water and sugar in a Pyrex saucepan. Add the vanilla bean and simmer briskly for about 12 minutes. Pare the pears and leave whole, with the stems left on. Place the pears in the syrup as they are peeled, to prevent them from turning brown. Have the syrup boiling as the pears are added. Turn them constantly when they are first put in. This will prevent them from browning on one side. Turn them for the first 5 minutes or so, then turn the fire below a simmer to poach. Test for doneness by piercing the pear with a cake tester or a sharp-pointed toothpick. When tender to the touch and a bit transparent all over they should have cooked enough. They are delicious served warm as well as chilled. Remove the vanilla bean before serving.

MORNING-AFTER-
HOG-BUTCHERING BREAKFAST

Black Raspberries and Cream

Eggs Sunny-Side Up

Oven-Cooked Fresh Bacon

Fried Sweetbreads

Country-Fried Apples

Biscuits—Corn Bread

Butter

Wild Strawberry Preserves—Wild Blackberry Jelly

Coffee

HOG KILLING

Hog killing was one of the special events of the year and generally took place in December—the exact time depending on a solid cold spell coinciding with the right time of the moon, which was when the moon was on the increase. The cold spell was essential, as the hogs could not be carved up until they were thoroughly chilled and the meat had firmed up enough to cut properly. This took a good three days of hanging in the open air.

Aside from the special feeding, fattening, and cleaning of the hogs that led up to the day of butchering, there were many other preparations to be made. Scaffolds for hanging the hogs had to be erected, and wood laid for the fires that would heat the iron drums of water needed for scalding and cleansing the hogs after they were killed. Many families had an outdoor or "summer" kitchen—an extra kitchen detached from the house which was used during the hot weather so that the continuous heat coming from a wood stove would not make the whole house unbearably hot. These summer kitchens were also useful at hog-killing time, as there was too much fat to be rendered, sausage meat to grind, and other cooking to handle easily in the main house, so they would be all scrubbed and put in order ahead of time.

The butchering day was a hectic one. Every family had a dozen or more hogs and we all joined in helping each other. After each hog was killed, it was carefully scalded so that the bristles would scrape off easily, leaving a smooth, unmarked skin. After this was done, the hind legs were fastened together by a special stock called a gambrel, which was shaped like a rolling pin with pointed ends. The stick was placed between the legs and the pointed ends were inserted under the hocks. To hang the hog, which would be about six feet long, two men would hoist it up, hooking the hind legs over the top of the scaffold. The hog was then cut down the center. A large, round tub was placed underneath for the entrails to fall into. My father would remove the liver and the bladder, which he would present to us. We would blow the bladders up with straws cut from reeds and hang them in the house to dry. By Christmas they would have turned transparent like beautiful balloons. We always handled them with care and made them part of our Christmas decorations.

The following morning my brothers and sisters and I would rush out before breakfast to see the hogs hanging from the scaffolds like giant statues. The hogs looked beautiful. They were glistening white inside with their lining of fat, and their skin was almost translucent after the scraping.

We waited with impatient excitement through the three days of hanging; we were all looking forward to the many delicious dishes that would be made after the hogs were cut up—fresh sausage, liver pudding, and the sweet, delicate tastes of fresh pork and bacon. One of my favorite foods that we always had after hog killing was crackling bread. When the lard was rendered and strained, little defatted pieces were left which we called cracklings. Cut into small pieces and mixed into cornmeal batter they made a bread which was deliciously crispy and chewy. Meanwhile, we enjoyed the fresh liver, which my mother would pan-fry for breakfast or dinner.

When the three-day period of hanging ended, the hogs were carved up. The special skill that was needed for butchering was provided by an itinerant hog-killer, who would always appear a few days before the first cold spell that we waited for so eagerly, and who would often stay on for three or four weeks past hog killing. (It was not unusual for someone to arrive for a few days' visit during the winter months and stay on for several weeks—sometimes until spring.)

As soon as the hogs were butchered, a series of necessary activities ensued that kept the whole community busy for at least a week or more. Besides all the special treats we would be enjoying at mealtime, it was the highly festive feeling of everyone working together that made this one of our favorite times in the year.

The first part of the hog to be removed was the layer of white fat that had seemed to glisten so when the hogs were hanging. This fat is known as leaf lard because it peels off in thin sheets or leaves. It is very special, as its taste and texture are so fine, and we always kept it and used it for pies, biscuits, and even cakes. A group of the women would be on hand to cut the lard into small cubes as soon as it was removed and then to render it in heavy iron pots. Sometimes the pots would be hung in a fork over an outdoor fire. The fat had to cook very slowly in order to turn liquid. Then it was strained and poured into 5-gallon tins. After it cooled, it was sealed and stored in a cool, dry place.

Each piece of meat had to be carved to a certain shape, and as it was cut, trimmings flowed from the hams, shoulders, and bacon. They would form a great pile and huge pots were needed to render this fat, which would be used for frying meats and other foods that didn't require the same fineness of flavor that pastry does. It took three or four days of constant work to render all of the lard, but when it was finished there would be a good year's supply for every family.

Among the trimmings there was always some lean as well as fat, and this had to be carefully cut away. The lean from the trimmings was put into the "sausage bin," along with what we now call loin. I think that was why the sausage was so good, because it had in it pieces from all parts of the hog. Lard and sausage meat are still being prepared in the same way in this part of Virginia.

Once the lard was rendered, the women would turn to making sausage (see page 206 for a recipe you can make at home). First our meat was seasoned with sage, black pepper, and salt, then it was ground in a sausage mill and made up into cakes and canned in jars, or stuffed into casings that came from the hogs' intestines and smoked. When all of the sausage had been cooked and sealed into jars, a piece of the jowl was cooked with the liver, then finely ground and seasoned with sage and onion. The jowl is mostly fat and makes the liver softer and lighter. We called this delicate pâté liver pudding, and it was a favorite dish. Some of the jowls were cured with the hams and bacon; they were delicious sliced and oven-fried for breakfast as a change from bacon.

While the women were busy with rendering the fat and cooking the sausage and liver, the men would prepare the hams, bacon, and shoulders. These would be seasoned with salt, black pepper, saltpeter, and brown sugar and stored in a wooden meat box for about six weeks. The meat would then be cleaned with a stiff brush and hung from hooks in the smokehouse, where it would be smoked for three or four days over green hickory logs and sassafras twigs.

After the meat had been smoked, it was put into clean, white bags and tied securely to make sure no flies or other insects got into the meat. It was then left to hang in the smokehouse until it was needed, which was usually late summer. Hams were sometimes left to age for a year or two. They become quite mellow and delicious when they are left this length of time and are usually saved for special events such as family reunions, weddings, and graduations.

Black Raspberries and Cream

Raspberries grew wild along the streams and edges of the nearby woodland and they ripened later in the season than strawberries. The black raspberries were particularly good for preserving because they remained firm, so we could have them as a treat, served with cream, throughout the winter and on into the spring. We preserved them in what seemed to me a most intriguing way. We would mix the berries with equal amounts of sugar and place them in glass bottles. Then we would cork the necks with a piece of cotton and pour melted wax over the tops. We would keep the filled bottles in an opening in the ground under a board in the kitchen floor and bring them out on special occasions like hog-butchering day because the flavor was so exotic. I have never forgotten the taste of them.

Eggs Sunny-Side Up

No breakfast was complete without eggs cooked in some form: boiled, poached, or fried. Even though we didn't have to buy them, they were greatly relished. Eggs of that day were fertile and had a real flavor. Of the various ways we cooked them—including wrapping them in wet brown paper and cooking them in the ashes of the fireplace—sunny side was the most elegant. They were more like a sunny-side soufflé. They were always fried in the same pan that the bacon or ham had just been cooked in, so they would absorb whatever flavor there was left in the pan. When fresh eggs were broken into the hot fat they held their shape, and the sizzling fat would cause them to cook quickly and to puff up. We would shake the pan around while they cooked so that the hot fat splashed over the whites and this would make the eggs puff into a ball. We would then serve them quickly while still puffy.

The same technique can be used with butter as well. Heat the butter to the foaming stage; put in the egg, and tilt the pan to one side so that the egg will be enveloped in the butter. When fully puffed, serve.

Bacon

Country breakfast bacon ranged from middling, jowl, shoulder to ham. Varying the cuts kept up a lively interest in each meal because every part tasted different—and I will never forget the taste of fresh bacon, sliced thin from the middling as soon as the meat was cold enough to carve, sprinkled with salt and fresh black pepper, whose aroma filled the air during hog-butchering time. The slices were placed in a hot skillet containing 2 tablespoons of lard, then set into the oven to cook for about 18 minutes. Fresh bacon should be cut from the section of the middling that is most fat. The lean part would be a bit tough.

The jowl, shoulder, and ham all have different flavors. They are first cured and then left hanging in the meat house. Each morning we would take a piece from the hook, place it on the workbench that was in the meat house, and with a sharp knife slice enough for breakfast, trimming away the rind from each thin slice. Returning to the kitchen, the slices were washed in a little warm water to take out excess salt, placed in a medium-hot frying pan, and set into a hot oven to cook. If bread was being baked the bacon would be placed on the floor of the oven. The slices could be turned if needed. If the bread finished baking first, the meat pan would be placed upon the rack in the oven. Total cooking time would be about,15 to 18 minutes, depending upon the thickness of the slices. This is an excellent way to cook very thin bacon, as I've said before; all kinds of bacon you buy today can be done this way. The over-all heat of the oven seems to completely relax the bacon, while giving it a crispy, chewy, baked flavor. When finished, remove from the oven and drain on brown paper.

Fried Pork Sweetbreads

There was very little meat for cooking immediately after hog butchering because all of the important pieces were put down in salt or ground into sausage and the liver went into pudding. But there was an assortment of organ meats, among them the sweetbreads, that were seasoned and put into an open baking pan and cooked in the oven. When everything was cooked, the contents of the pan was all brown and aromatic. I remember tasting the sweetbreads as a child, and they were delicious to me; I never forgot the flavor. I was disappointed later when I tried veal sweetbreads, expecting them to be brown and crisp like those we did. It would be hard to duplicate that dish now, but one can prepare delicious, crisp sweetbreads.

Serves 5 to 6

2 pounds pork sweetbreads (or if available, veal)
1 cup fresh bread crumbs, sifted fine
2 eggs, beaten
½ cup flour
½ teaspoon salt
½ teaspoon black pepper
½ cup (1 stick) butter
1 lemon, cut in wedges
¼ cup finely cut parsley

To prepare, wash the sweetbreads well in cold water, then plunge into boiling salted water for about 10 minutes. Then plunge into cold water, drain, and wipe dry. Place in freezer compartment for about 15 minutes to become firm enough to remove outer web and slice well into ¼-inch slices. Coat the slices in about two-thirds of the cup of fresh bread crumbs, and then in beaten egg, then in a mixture of flour, salt and pepper, and the remaining bread crumbs. Fry in butter a few minutes on each side and drain on brown paper. Serve hot, garnished with lemon wedges and finely cut parsley.

√Country-Fried Apples

6 apples   *Serves 5 to 6*
3 tablespoons fresh bacon fat
⅓ cup sugar

Prepare apples by peeling, quartering, coring, and quartering again. Heat the bacon fat in a hot skillet and when sizzling add the apples. Cover and cook briskly until the apples become soft and there is juice in the pan. Timing depends upon the kind of apple you use, but you can tell the apples are soft when they begin to break up. Remove cover and sprinkle the sugar over the apples. Stir and cook with the cover off until the liquid has dried up and apples begin to brown. Cook medium-brisk until the apples are quite brown. Stir frequently. The apples should be a mixture of light and very dark amber.

For recipe for **Biscuits,** see page 124.

Corn Bread

2 cups sifted white cornmeal   *Serves 5 to 6*
½ teaspoon salt
½ teaspoon baking soda
2 teaspoons Royal Baking Powder
3 eggs, beaten
1 tablespoon lard
1 tablespoon butter
2 cups sour milk, or buttermilk

9 x 10-inch pan

Sift cornmeal, salt, soda, and baking powder into a mixing bowl.
Stir in the beaten eggs. At this point set the baking pan in the oven
with the lard and butter added. Pour the sour milk into the cornmeal
batter and stir well. Now remove the pan from the oven and tilt it
all around to oil the whole surface of the pan. Pour off into the batter
what fat remains. Mix well and pour the batter into the hot pan.
Cornmeal batter must be poured into a sizzling hot pan, otherwise it
will stick. Bake at 400° for 25 to 30 minutes. Remove and cut into
squares. Serve hot.

Note: Sometimes we would add a tablespoon of lard to the baking
pan and return it to the oven to heat. Then we would pour the batter
in, forcing the extra fat into the corners of the pan. (When cooked,
the corner pieces of bread would have a lacy, crispy edge and there
would be quite a bit of competition for those pieces when it was
placed on the table.)

Hog-butchering breakfast was the kind of occasion when we
would open some of the wild strawberry preserves we had made in
mid-May (see page 22) and the wild blackberry jelly we had put up
in July (see page 89).

PREPARATIONS FOR CHRISTMAS

Hickory Nut Cookies

Fall was harvest time for the squirrels as well and there would be a race between us and the squirrels for the wild hickory nuts. They could carry the crop of a tree away in one afternoon. Hickory trees are very tall so we had to wait until the nuts fell to the ground. Also, the fallen ones would be the ripe ones. The squirrels seemed to have known this, too.

Once the nuts were gathered, we couldn't decide whether to use them in cooking or just keep them as they were. But we made special things usually. We mixed the nuts into fruitcake or cookies after the painstaking job of cracking them and picking out the tiny bits of meat.

Hickory nuts can be found in most dried fruit and nut shops that cater to home bakers and interested persons.

Two or three days before you plan to make these cookies, fill a pint jar with either powdered or extrafine sugar and stick a fresh vanilla bean in the center. Cap tightly. The cookies will keep for Christmas.

> 2 cups grated hickory nuts
> 1¾ cups sifted all-purpose flour
> 1 cup soft butter
> ¼ cup sugar
> Pinch of salt
> 1 teaspoon almond extract
> 1 teaspoon vanilla extract
> Vanilla sugar (see above)

Preheat oven to 350°. Either chop the nuts fine or put them through a nut grater and measure. Handle them lightly so they don't pack down. Sift flour once. Beat the butter, sugar, and salt together until the sugar has dissolved and the texture is creamy. Add flavorings.

Beating at a low speed, gradually add the flour. When flour has been well blended, mix in the nuts. If your kitchen is very warm, chill the dough until it is easy to handle. Using your fingers, shape the dough into 1-inch balls or crescents and place them on ungreased cookie sheets. Bake until lightly browned, about 15 to 20 minutes.

Remove cookies onto cake racks to cool for about 15 minutes before rolling them in the vanilla sugar. When they are cold, store them in a cookie tin. If you made vanilla sugar with powdered sugar and it is absorbed by the cookies, sift a little more over the cookies before serving.

Christmas Fruitcake

Late September was a fine time to make the Christmas fruitcake. There were rainy days in September when outside work was curtailed and the cookstove was on, making the kitchen warm and cozy. The family was around and friends were dropping in—chopping fruit, grinding spices, and sampling homemade wine, trying to decide which one was best for the cake, and sipping a bit of whiskey as well. Preparing the cake became a festive occasion, and almost as exciting as Christmas itself. In selecting ingredients for the fruitcake, it is best to buy a few important items such as citron, seeded raisins, and candied peel in late December for the following Christmas. The freshest ingredients come into the market too late to make an aged cake. The special fruits can be kept perfectly well in a cool, dry place (not a refrigerator) until it's time to make the cake. The same care should be taken with spices. Cinnamon from Ceylon is much more delicate and sweet than the other bark that is found today at most fancy food places. Fruitcake is so special and lasts so long that only the best ingredients should be used in it.

2 cups (1 pound) butter
2 cups granulated sugar
2 cups soft brown sugar (not brownulated)
10 medium-sized eggs, well beaten
1 cup unsulphured molasses
1 cup sorghum molasses
1 cup grape jelly
1 cup blackberry wine
2 teaspoons freshly ground Ceylon cinnamon
⅔ nutmeg, grated
2 teaspoons freshly ground mace
2 teaspoons freshly ground allspice
1 teaspoon freshly ground cloves
2 tablespoons vanilla extract
8 cups sifted unbleached flour

Makes about 17 pounds of batter for 2 large cakes

4 teaspoons Royal Baking Powder

2 pounds seeded muscat raisins (seed by hand preferably)

2 pounds seedless dark raisins

1 pound citron, sliced thin and cut into ½-inch pieces

1 pound currants

½ pound each candied orange and lemon peel (can be made at home)

2 cups rum or old brandy

2 10-inch tube pans, greased and lined with uncontaminated brown paper well-greased on both sides. Line the pans on bottom and sides.

Cream the butter and sugars until light. Add beaten eggs and mix well while stirring in molasses, jelly, and wine. Stir in spices, vanilla, and flour with baking powder added. Add in the fruit bit by bit, stirring well after each addition. When well mixed, spoon the batter into the tube pans. Fill three quarters full and set the pans in an odorless, cold place for 2 days. Then set the cake batter into a preheated oven that ranges between 250° and 300° for 4 hours. Remove from oven and cool in pans. When cold, remove from pans and leave cakes encased in paper wrapping; store in clean, dry tins or wooden boxes. (Any container other than plastic.) Lace the cakes beginning in early December once a week with ½ cup rum or old brandy. Lace for 4 weeks. Keep the containers covered.

Note: The best shop in New York City for fruit and some spices is H. Roth and Sons.

Mincemeat

We always made our mincemeat three or four weeks before Christmas and stored it in a big stone crock. It would keep a year or more —but it was always eaten up during the winter.

½ pound bottom round of beef
2 ounces suet (from veal kidney is best)
2 ounces currants
1 ounce seedless raisins
1 ounce seeded raisins
1 ounce candied lemon peel
1 ounce candied orange peel
1 cup finely chopped tart apples
3½ ounces soft brown sugar
½ teaspoon each cinnamon, allspice, cloves,
   ginger
½ nutmeg, grated
½ teaspoon salt
½ cup each Madeira, rum, and brandy

*Makes about
8 cups*

1 ½-gallon stone crock, or bowl or glass jars
   of approximately same quantity

Place the beef in a saucepan of boiling water just enough to cover. Simmer the meat 1 hour until tender, remove from burner, and leave to become really cold. Then chop fine and put through a meat grinder. Remove skin from suet and chop by hand until it becomes almost as smooth as lard. In a large mixing bowl mix the fruits well with a clean wooden spoon. Sprinkle over the brown sugar and spices, salt, and suet. Continue to stir. Pour together the rum, Madeira, and brandy. Add chopped beef to fruit mixture, sprinkle over the rum mixture, and stir well. Spoon the mixture into the clean 5-gallon stone jar or smaller glass jars. Tie over with a heavy, clean cloth. Store in a cold, dry place for 3 to 4 weeks.

Winter

CHRISTMAS

Around Christmastime the kitchens of Freetown would grow fragrant with the baking of cakes, fruit puddings, cookies, and candy. Exchanging gifts was not a custom at that time, but we did look forward to hanging our stockings from the mantel and finding them filled on Christmas morning with tasty "imported" nuts from Lahore's, our favorite hard candies with the cinnamon-flavored red eye, and oranges whose special Christmas aroma reached us at the top of the stairs. And for us four girls, there would also be little celluloid dolls with movable arms and legs that we so loved, and new paper dolls with their fascinating clip-on wardrobes. But mainly getting ready for Christmas meant preparing all kinds of delicious foods that we would enjoy with our families and friends during the days between Christmas Eve and New Year's Day.

There was a special excitement in the kitchens, as many of the things we prepared were foods we tasted only at Christmas. This was the only time in the year when we had oranges, almonds, Brazil nuts, and raisins that came in clusters. And although we were miles from the sea, at Christmas one of the treats we always looked forward to was oysters. The oysters were delivered to Lahore's in barrels on Christmas Eve day, and late on Christmas Eve we would climb the steps over the pasture fence and walk along the path through the woods to the store, carrying our covered tin pails. Mr. Jackson, the storekeeper, would fill some of our pails with oysters. And before we left he always filled our hands with nuts and candy.

We were excited by all the preparations for Christmas, but my own favorite chores were chopping the nuts and raisins for Mother and stirring the wonderful-smelling dark mixtures of fruits and brandy that would go into the fruitcake and plum pudding, and decorating the house with evergreens.

Just before Christmas a green lacy vine called running cedar appeared in the woods around Freetown and we would gather yards and yards of it. We draped everything in the house with it: windows, doors, even the large gilded frames that held the pictures of each of my aunts and uncles. We picked the prickly branches of a giant holly tree—the largest holly I've ever seen—which grew on the top of a nearby hill, and we cut armloads of pine boughs and juniper. My mother always gave the fireplace and hearth a fresh white-washing the day before Christmas, and washed, starched, and ironed the white lace curtains. On Christmas Eve my father would set up the tree in one corner of the room and we would decorate it with pink, white, and blue strings of popcorn that we had popped, dipped in colored sugar water, and carefully threaded. Small white candles nestled on tufts of cotton were the last decorations to be placed on the tree.

I loved the way the greens looked set off by the white hearth and walls and the stiff white curtains which they draped. In the evenings the soft orange glow from the fire and from the candlelight and the fragrance of the cedar and juniper mingling with the smell of chestnuts roasting always made me wish that Christmas week would last until spring, though I suspected that my mother did not share my wish.

The celebration of Christmas Day began before daybreak with the shooting off of Roman candles. With a great roaring noise they exploded into balls of red fire arcing into the still-dark sky. After they had all been set off, my father would light sparklers for us. We could never imagine Christmas without Roman candles and sparklers; for us it was the most important part of the whole day.

Finally we would go back into the warmth of the house for breakfast. There would be eggs and sausages and plates of hot biscuits with my mother's best preserves, and pan-fried oysters which would taste so sweet, crispy, and delicious. The familiar smell of hot coffee and cocoa mixed with the special aroma of bourbon, which was part of every holiday breakfast. We were allowed to smell, but never to taste this special drink of the menfolk.

We all dressed in our Sunday dresses for Christmas dinner. Dinner was at noon so that we would be finished in time for the men to feed the animals before dark. My mother would have been in the kitchen since five o'clock and half of the night as well, and when the dinner was ready we would gather round the table and sit for hours enjoying all the things she had prepared.

Christmas week was spent visiting back and forth, as at this time of year the men were able to take off some time. The women enjoyed tasting each other's baking and the men took pleasure in comparing the wines they had made at harvest time—wild plum, elderberry, dandelion, and grape. And they usually managed to enjoy a taste of that bourbon as well.

Every household had a sideboard or a food safe, and these would be laden throughout the week with all the foods that had been made for the holiday. Ours would hold baked ham, smothered rabbit, a pan of mixed small birds that had been trapped in the snow, braised guinea hen, liver pudding, and sometimes a roasted wild turkey that had grown up with our own flock (but usually a fat roast hen), and all the sweet and pungent pickles my mother had made from cucumbers and watermelon rind, crab apples and peaches. The open shelf of the sideboard would be lined with all the traditional holiday cakes: caramel and coconut layer cakes, pound cake, and my mother's rich, dark, flavorful fruitcake. There were plates of fudge and peanut brittle and crocks filled with crisp sugar cookies. The food safe was filled with mince pies, and fruit pies made with the canned fruit of summer.

Although there were no exceptions to our usual custom of sitting down together three times a day for meals, during Christmas week we were free to return to the food safe as many times a day as we liked and my mother would never say a word. But at the end of holiday week we were all given a home-brewed physic which was really vile! It was so vile I've never quite forgotten the taste of it.

On New Year's Day when all the Christmas decorations were taken down, we felt sad and let down; to us our house looked drab and naked, and although the visiting back and forth would continue until winter came to an end, Christmas was over.

CHRISTMAS EVE SUPPER

Oyster Stew

Baked Country Ham

Scalloped Potatoes

Pan-Braised Spareribs

Crusty Yeast Bread—Ham Biscuits

Wild Blackberry Jelly—Watermelon-Rind Pickles

Yellow Vanilla Pound Cake—Hickory Nut Cookies—Sugar Cookies

Dandelion Wine—Plum Wine

Coffee

A typical Christmas Eve supper would be very light for us children and nervously eaten because of our anxiousness to go to sleep and wake up very early to see what Santa had left in our stockings for us. We wouldn't eat much more than the oyster stew made from the first oysters of the season and crispy biscuits, but the grownups had a good time putting together special things and eating plentifully.

Oyster Stew

1 quart oysters   *Serves 8*
1½ tablespoons butter
3 cups scalded milk
1 cup heavy cream
¼ teaspoon cayenne pepper
⅛ teaspoon nutmeg
Salt
Chopped parsley

Drain the oysters. Melt 1 tablespoon of the butter in a hot skillet, then add the oysters, turning them on both sides until they begin to curl. Pour in the scalded milk and transfer the mixture to a saucepan. Pour the cream into the skillet and boil rapidly until reduced by one half, then add the reduced cream to the oyster mixture and heat on a medium flame; do not boil. Add cayenne, nutmeg, and salt to taste, and just before serving add ½ tablespoon butter. Serve when hot and garnish with chopped parsley.

For recipe for **Baked Virginia Ham,** see page 32.

Scalloped Potatoes

2 pounds white potatoes   *Serves 8*
Freshly ground black pepper
½ cup (1 stick) butter
1 pint beef bouillon

1 2-quart casserole, buttered

Peel and slice raw potatoes thin. Layer them in the buttered casserole. Sprinkle each layer with freshly ground black pepper and dot over with butter. Repeat the process until casserole is filled. Arrange the top layer in a circle or rectangular design according to the design of the dish. Pour in enough bouillon to reach just under the top layer of the potatoes. Dot the top liberally with butter and set in center of an oven preheated to 350°. Bake for 60 minutes. When finished, the dish has a nice crusty top.

Note: The casserole may be rubbed with garlic if desired. Also, the layers of potatoes may be sprinkled with finely chopped onion.

Pan-Braised Spareribs

When purchasing spareribs try to get them without the tips—that is the meaty part of the bottom of the ribs. Most often it is too tough and requires longer cooking than the rest of the ribs.

Have the butcher cut away the tips and crack the ribs through the middle but not into two pieces.

3 pounds spareribs *Serves 4 to 5*

MARINADE
3 tablespoons brown sugar
5 tablespoons honey
⅔ cup soy sauce
1 teaspoon salt
6 tablespoons sweet sherry
½ cup strained chili sauce
½ tablespoon finely chopped fresh ginger root
1 or 2 cloves garlic, crushed

GLAZE
¼ cup soy sauce
¼ cup honey

Mix marinade ingredients together well.

For best results, cook spareribs first by parboiling. Place the ribs in a rectangular pan with just enough water to be level with the ribs, simmer just until tender, about 1½ hours. Remove ribs from pan and cool. When cool enough to handle, brush each piece of sparerib over with marinade. Place in deep dish and leave to marinate for 1 hour, no longer. The spices will break down if held longer. Preheat oven to 425°. Lay the sheets of spareribs on a pan containing a wire rack and set into the oven, turning it down to 350° to crisp for no more than 20 minutes. Remove from oven and paint with mixture of soy sauce and honey. Return to oven and cook for 4 to 5 minutes only. Remove and cut into serving portions.

For recipe for **Crusty Yeast Bread,** see page 46.

For recipe for **Wild Blackberry Jelly,** see page 89.

For recipe for **Watermelon-Rind Pickles,** see page 91.

For recipe for **Yellow Vanilla Pound Cake,** see page 63.

For recipe for **Hickory Nut Cookies,** see page 190.

For recipe for **Sugar Cookies,** see page 88.

For recipe for **Dandelion Wine,** see page 26.

For recipe for **Plum Wine,** see page 99.

CHRISTMAS BREAKFAST

Pan-Fried Oysters

Eggs Sunny-Side Up

Liver Pudding

Pork Sausage

Skillet-Fried Potatoes

Biscuits

Butter

Wild Strawberry Preserves

Bourbon

Coffee

Christmas breakfast was one to be remembered. While the activities of setting off the sparklers and Roman candles were going on, the house was filled with the aroma of frying oysters, coffee, and baking bread. A fine way to begin this special day.

Pan-Fried Oysters

4 eggs, beaten   *Serves 4 to 5*
1 teaspoon salt
2 tablespoons peanut oil
2 cups plain cracker meal
1 quart drained oysters
Fresh lard

Place the eggs in a bowl, add salt, beat well with a fork, and add in the peanut oil. Place a cup of cracker meal on a sheet of wax paper. With a fork, pick up each oyster, dip it into the egg mixture, and place it upon the cracker meal. To bread the oyster shift the wax paper. Place each oyster on a second plain sheet of wax paper as it is breaded and let stand a few minutes before frying. To fry, heat an aluminum skillet with ½ cup lard; when it reaches the smoking point, put oysters in and fry them until they turn a golden brown, about 2 minutes on each side. Drain the oysters on a piece of brown paper and serve while hot and crispy.

For recipe for **Eggs Sunny-Side Up,** see page 185.

Liver Pudding

Liver pudding was one of the things we all loved best at hog butchering. The liver was cut first and hung in the cold open air for 4 or 5 days to chill while we did all the chores of grinding sausage, storing away the meats, and rendering the lard. The stove was then free to cook the liver pudding. Ingredients used in making the pudding were not unusual. It was the feed and care given the pigs and the method of preparing the pudding that made it so delicious. We always made huge amounts, some to give away and the rest to store so it would last throughout the winter to be served on special mornings for breakfast.We kept it by setting it into the spring box or the meat house on a low shelf to keep cool.

The liver would be cut away from the hasslet or lungs and put into a large pot along with an equal amount of jowl, which is a very fatty piece of the pig. In fact, jowl was the secret to the pudding being so light and creamy. The rest is simple, as you can see, and can be made—almost as good—from what you buy in the market.

> 1½ pounds fresh pork liver
> 1½ pounds fresh pork jowl, or 1½ pounds fresh,
>   unsalted pork middling or uncured bacon
> 1 medium onion
> 2 cups liquid from boiled liver mixture
> 2 teaspoons salt
> ½ teaspoon freshly ground black pepper
> 1 teaspoon fresh-purchased sage
>
> *1 heavy tin loaf pan, or 1 2½-quart casserole*

The liver should not be sliced; leave it in one piece. The jowl should be in one piece as well, and is cooked in the skin. If fresh bacon or middling is used, the lean is removed. Place the liver, jowl, and onion in a pot with enough cold water to cover about 2 inches above the meat. Set to cook on a medium-high burner until the pot begins to simmer. Cook gently until the jowl is tender, about 2 hours. Remove the meat and onion from pot and leave to cool. Cut the liver and jowl with their skins into small pieces and put them through a food chopper or meat grinder along with the onion. Alternate fat and liver to keep the mill from clogging up. When all is ground, add 2 cups of the liquid from the cooked liver mixture. Pour off the top water and use the bottom liquid because it contains residue from the cooked meat. Stir the liver mixture; you will have a very liquid batter. Then add in salt, pepper, and sage. Mix well and pour into a heavy tin loaf pan or 2-quart casserole. Bake in a preheated 250° oven for 2½ hours until the pudding has completely dried down. If not cooked enough, the pudding will not slice properly. It is the long cooking that develops the fine flavor of the pudding. Remove from oven. When cool, place in cold place or in refrigerator.

Note: Instead of using a food chopper, after cooking and cooling I have grated the liver on the largest side of a four-sided grater, then put it into a blender using fat and liquid in small batches until the mixture is all blended.

Whole pork, liver, fresh bacon, and jowl can be found in German or Latin neighborhoods, and in some good butcher shops where fresh pork is available.

Pork Sausage

Sausage was just as popular as liver pudding. At butchering time we looked forward to the morning when we would be served the first sausage cakes of the season, well-seasoned, light, and springy in texture. The key to their goodness was the meat from our hand-raised hogs, home-grown spices, freshly ground black pepper, and an extra amount of fat, which is what makes a light sausage cake.

You can make sausage successfully at home today if you purchase some pork from the loin and fresh green bacon (unsalted) for extra fat. Fresh bacon can be found readily in Spanish and European communities in most big cities.

> 3 pounds fresh lean pork (from loin and
>   shoulder)
> 4 pounds fresh fat pork trimming from loin and
>   green bacon with rind cut off
> 1½ tablespoons salt (or to taste)
> 2 teaspoons fresh-ground black pepper

2 teaspoons crushed dried sage
¼ teaspoon cayenne pepper
½ tablespoon lard

Sausage mill or meat grinder

First, cut the pieces of lean and fat meat into ½-inch strips to make it easier to feed the machine. Then sprinkle pieces of meat with the salt, pepper, sage and cayenne pepper. Mix well together and feed into the machine, alternating fat and lean; if you add fat alone, you will clog the machine. When all of the meat has been ground, fry a small amount to test for salt. Add more if you like it saltier, but the real flavor of the sausage will not be reached until after a day of aging. The sausage can be made into cakes the size of biscuits (½ inch thick and about 2½ inches in diameter). Wrap them in heavy wax paper, place in foil, and store in freezer until needed.

To fry, put ½ tablespoon lard into a hot frying pan and brown the cakes on each side. Cooking time should be about 15 minutes, uncovered. Or you can cook them for the same amount of time in a 350° oven. When cooked, drain on clean paper towel to remove excess fat. Serve hot.

Thin-Sliced Skillet-Fried White Potatoes

5 medium-sized old potatoes　　　　　*Serves 5 to 6*
4 tablespoons butter
Salt
Freshly ground pepper

1 12-inch skillet with cover

Use old potatoes, preferably. Peel and slice thin with a vegetable slicer. Slicing can be done by hand but it is difficult to keep each slice uniformly thin. Have ready skillet with cover. Heat the skillet until hot, and add 4 tablespoons butter. When the butter is melted and at the foaming stage, add in the sliced potatoes. Spread them uniformly over the pan. Cover and cook briskly. In about 3 minutes turn with a cake turner. Turn the whole batch over, bringing the brown ones to the top. Continue this process until most of the potatoes are brown, shifting the brown pieces to one side. A few minutes before they are finished cooking, remove the lid to let them dry out. Serve hot, sprinkled with salt and pepper.

For recipe for **Biscuits,** see page 124.

For recipe for **Wild Strawberry Preserves,** see page 22.

Bourbon

About bourbon, I was an authority on the smell of it. Grandpa always presided over the bottle of bourbon that Uncle George brought from New York. Exposing a bottle of whiskey just wasn't done. As children, all we ever saw were the little glasses being passed to the guests, and on special occasions the little glasses would appear on the breakfast table. All I ever remember seeing was the sugar left in the bottom of the glass, and the divine aroma filling the room. That bourbon smell became associated with Uncle George and other festive occasions, along with the aroma of a cigar that only Uncle George brought.

CHRISTMAS DINNER

Roast Chicken with Dressing
Whipped White Potatoes
Baked Rabbit
Steamed Wild Watercress
Lima Beans in Cream
Spiced Seckel Pears
Sweet Cucumber Pickles
Grape Jelly
Biscuits
Hot Mince Pie
Persimmon Pudding with Clear Sauce
Fruitcake
Coconut Layer Cake
Caramel Fudge—Chocolate Fudge
Divinity Cream
Popcorn
Bowl of Oranges, Raisin Clusters, Brazil Nuts, Almonds
Blackberry Wine
Coffee

Christmas dinner was the more sober meal. A feast of winter har-
vest, it would consist of roast meat from hog butchering, a fat, old
hen stuffed and roasted to a turn, rabbits and birds aged from hunt-
ing season, vegetables from summer canning, pickles, relishes, pre-
serves, and jellies to go with the rich meat. There were pies, cakes,
and puddings to last throughout the season. That was the time when
the spirit of giving began. After dinner, platters of food began to be
exchanged throughout Freetown.

A Good Chicken

Nothing pleased us more than to have a big, fat hen for a holiday
meal. Turkeys were raised for the city holiday market as a late cash
crop. At the end of winter the turkey hens began to lay and it was
our job to watch them and to find their nests, which were either
along the fence row or in the edge of the woods under a pile of brush.
If they thought we were watching them they would never go to the
nest, or they would just squat down the moment we took our eyes
from them. Mother would turn them out the next day and send us
right back until we saw where they went into the thicket. When we
found the nest, Mother would take a china egg and put it there in
place of the turkey eggs; after that we would go every day to pick up
the eggs. When the turkey hens decided to set, the eggs would be
replaced and a coop, placed over the hen, would be carefully fastened down to keep out such animals as foxes or stray dogs. The
hen would be fed and watered and when the turkey poults hatched
there was another chore. The one I remember most was days when
a thunderstorm was approaching and we were supposed to bring
them to the coop from the field. But the mother hen would just sit
down to keep us from finding her, with the storm fast approaching.
Somehow we would finally get them into their coops. Life on the
farm had its hectic moments; heaven help us if the baby turkeys
had drowned.

After the struggle to raise them to maturity, we had to dress them for the market, which meant to dry-pick them after they were killed. We always picked the feathers dry while the turkey was warm. They were hung in a shed to chill, then packed and shipped to Philadelphia. By that time we were quite happy to relax and have a nice holiday dinner without turkey.

The type of domestic hens we raised weighed sometimes as much as ten pounds, so a hen stuffed with sage seasoning, parboiled and roasted, was perfectly delicious, along with side dishes of game or pork. Even though we raised many chickens, we would save a special hen for a special meal. Some hens grew larger than others; usually they would be no less than a year old. Another interesting feature was the eggs inside of the hen. If we made chicken stew the eggs were dropped in. It was so appetizing to see a big bowl of chicken with a dozen yellow yolks in the sauce. The older hens were more flavorful, which was a most important aspect, and this would be discussed for days to come.

Most of the chickens today are raised in apartment houses and live out their lives without ever touching the ground. This type of rearing renders them too soft for the taste of someone who has experienced eating chickens raised on the ground and then placed in a pen with a wire floor to cleanse them before dressing them.

Today you just have to shop around for a good chicken. I have found Perdue one of the best commercial growers, and chickens in health-food stores are often superior—if you can afford them.

Roast Chicken with Dressing

DRESSING *Serves 5 to 6*

6 cups finely cubed dry bread crumbs, cut from
    dry bread
⅔ cup finely cubed celery
2 tablespoons finely cut celery leaves
½ cup finely cubed onion
1 teaspoon salt
1 teaspoon fresh-ground black pepper
½ teaspoon fresh or dried thyme, rubbed to
    powder
2 teaspoons crushed, fresh sage leaves
6 ounces (1½ sticks) melted butter

1 roasting hen, or capon, 6 to 8 pounds
Soft butter

The fresh onion and celery make a very aromatic stuffing. Combine dressing ingredients, except butter, in a large mixing bowl and mix well. Pour over the melted butter and mix well again. I find it better not to moisten the crumbs, as the juice from the celery and onion plus the liquid from the hen will be just enough to moisten the stuffing.

To prepare for roasting, wash the chicken well under cold water, but don't soak it. After washing, wipe dry inside and out with a damp cloth and fill with the bread-crumb dressing. Stitch the opening with a needle and white thread, tie the legs in place, and rub the chicken over with soft butter. Set into a preheated 425° oven, close the door, and turn the temperature back to 375°. After 40 minutes of cooking there should be quite a bit of liquid in the roasting pan (and even more so when roasting a chicken without stuffing). Remove the chicken from the oven, baste it, and then pour the liquid contents from the pan into a bowl. Return it to the oven and continue roasting, basting every 20 minutes with a bit of soft butter. Continue to pour the liquid contents from the roasting pan into the bowl. In the meantime, while the chicken is still cooking, skim off all of the fat from the top of the liquid in the bowl. When the chicken is done—it should be well-cooked and crisp in about 1½ hours—remove it from the pan. Pour in the liquid from the bowl, heat the pan over the burner, running a spoon around the pan to dislodge all particles, let the sauce boil quickly and briefly to thicken, and pour through a strainer into a sauceboat. See that it is kept hot until served. I caution against adding water; it too often spoils the flavor. If water is used it shouldn't be more than a tablespoonful.

The reason for pouring away the liquid from the chicken while it is roasting is to save the very fine essence that is being extracted from the chicken as it cooks. Otherwise it will quickly evaporate because of the heat, and all that will be left in the pan will be fat— and that should be poured off and water added. The chicken should be served as soon as removed from the oven, while the skin is hot and crispy. This can be done if the rest of the meal is planned to be ready in time with the chicken.

Whipped White Potatoes

> 5 to 6 medium-sized Idaho potatoes
> 1 teaspoon salt
> ¼ cup (½ stick) butter
> ½ teaspoon freshly ground white pepper
> 1 cup hot milk
> 2 teaspoons freshly cut parsley, or some finely
>   cut chives

Wash and pare the potatoes and cut them in half. Place them in a saucepan and pour in boiling water to cover. Add the salt and cook briskly for 20 minutes.

Drain and mash with a potato masher or put them through a Foley mill. Add the butter, pepper, and salt to taste. Pour in the hot milk and beat well by hand or with an electric mixer until the potatoes are light and fluffy.

Spoon the mixture into a heated casserole, dot with butter, and set under the broiler to slightly brown the peaks. Sprinkle over with the parsley or chives and serve piping hot.

Baked Rabbit

During the hunting season, a variety of game was bagged. Rabbit was the most plentiful and it kept very well. Most game can be kept, once the insides are removed, for a long period of time without being treated. We always left it hanging in fur or feathers during the winter and there was always a rabbit for Christmas. We cooked it various ways, according to its age and tenderness. Baked in the wood cook oven was one way we loved it. It was simple, rich, and fine-flavored.

1 3- to 4-pound rabbit   *Serves 4 to 5*
1 tablespoon soft butter
Salt and pepper
½ teaspoon thyme
1 to 2 tablespoons flour
2 to 3 slices smoked shoulder or bacon
1 medium onion, sliced
1 cup water

Wipe the rabbit with a damp cloth, place it in a baking pan, rub butter over, sprinkle with salt, pepper, thyme, and a light sifting of flour. Place 2 or 3 slices of smoked shoulder of pork or bacon over the rabbit, a sliced onion, and spill a cup of water over. Cover the pan and set into a 350° oven for an hour and a half, opening the oven and basting every 15 to 20 minutes. When cooked, carve the rabbit and place on a platter.

Dress the rabbit if it is your own game; with a store-bought rabbit, that won't be necessary.

Steamed Wild Watercress

Several varieties of watercress grew in our area. There was a type called malecress, which no one would eat. A very small leafy variety grew inside small streams and in bottomlands, as well as in uplands. The cress most commonly used was a completely flat plant that grew best under snow and in very cold weather. It was quite peppery and a bit bitter. It was widely used both as a tonic and as a food. Since African diet is based on nutrition, it was a natural part of our heritage to pick and eat that which was found to make one feel better. This watercress gave off a high aroma as it was cooked and the flavor was a bit more wholesome than some of the other leafy greens of other areas. We gathered it in large quantities, hung it in the meat house, and used it as needed. The hothouse cress one sees in the market, used as a garnish and in salads, can be cooked as a change from spinach, the cultivated type being more tender. It can be steamed or cooked in hot oil.

My favorite is the uncultivated. Wash it carefully, as it is usually very gritty, cut some of the root away and some of the tough stem. Gently boil a piece of smoked meat. When completely tender, add the cress and cook gently for 45 minutes. Drain and serve as other greens.

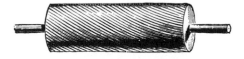

Lima Beans in Cream

1½ pints shelled green limas   *Serves 4 to 5*
½ pint heavy cream
1 scant teaspoon salt
¼ teaspoon freshly ground black pepper
2 teaspoons butter

Place the lima beans in a saucepan of boiling water that covers the beans by 2 inches. Cover the pan loosely and boil briskly (35 to 45 minutes) until the beans are completely tender. Drain away the liquid and pour in the heavy cream. Sprinkle in salt and freshly ground pepper. Stir by shaking the pan. Let the beans and cream heat without boiling until ready to serve. Add butter and serve hot. They are delicious.

For recipe for **Spiced Seckel Pears,** see page 90.

For recipe for **Cucumber Pickles,** see page 94.

For recipe for **Grape Jelly,** see page 162.

For recipe for **Biscuits,** see page 124.

Hot Mince Pie

PASTRY
2 cups sifted flour
½ teaspoon salt
½ cup cold lard
¼ cup cold water

FILLING
2 cups mincemeat (page 194)

Treat the same way as other two-crust pie pastries, page 41. Fill and bake for 50 minutes at 350°. Serve hot.

Persimmon Pudding

Uncultivated persimmons are more delicious after a frost has fallen on them—and the ones around us were at their best just about Christmastime. Uncultivated ones are not as juicy but they are more tasty and darker when frostbitten.

4 ounces suet   *Serves 4 to 5*

⅔ cup fresh-grated bread crumbs, without
    the crust

½ cup hot milk

1 packed cup brown sugar

¼ cup flour

3 eggs, separated

¼ teaspoon salt

1 teaspoon cinnamon

1 teaspoon fresh-grated nutmeg

½ teaspoon mace

4 large cultivated persimmons (triple the
    number if using wild)

¼ cup rum

2 teaspoons Royal Baking Powder

Remove all tissue and skin from the suet and chop it finely with a chopping knife. Remove the crust from enough slices of white bread to make ⅔ cup grated. Grating bread against the large holes of a four-sided grater makes much lighter crumbs; it is quick and easy, too. Put the crumbs into a mixing bowl. Pour the hot milk over the crumbs and leave them to stand a few minutes. Add the chopped suet, mix well, add sugar and flour and stir. Beat the egg yolks, add, and stir well again. Add salt, cinnamon, nutmeg, and mace. Stir after each addition. Cut the persimmons in half, remove the seeds, and scoop out the pulp. You should have about 2½ cups; add it to the suet-crumb mixture. Add rum and baking powder. Lastly, beat egg whites until stiff, fold in, and spoon the mixture into a pudding mold. Cover and set into a container of boiling water. Steam for 1½ hours. Remove from burner, leave to cool in mold. Reheat by steaming again on a slow burner for 1 hour. Serve hot with a clear sauce.

CLEAR SAUCE
⅔ cup sugar
Pinch of salt
2 teaspoons cornstarch
¼ teaspoon grated nutmeg
1 cup boiling water
3 tablespoons brandy

Mix sugar, salt, cornstarch, and nutmeg together in a non-aluminum saucepan. Pour in the boiling water, stirring constantly. Set on a medium-low burner and simmer for 12 minutes. Reheat and add brandy before serving.

For recipe for **Fruitcake,** see page 192.

Coconut Layer Cake

Coconut layer cake was one of the most famous desserts we baked. Coconuts were only available at Christmas, so that was the only time we could enjoy a feathery light coconut cake; other times it was topped with dried coconut. The batter was mixed with great care. When the cake was baked and frosted it was sprinkled generously with the sweet, grated coconut.

¼ teaspoon salt
3 teaspoons Royal Baking Powder
2 cups sifted all-purpose unbleached flour
½ cup (1 stick) butter
1¼ cups finely granulated sugar
2 egg yolks, beaten
2 teaspoons vanilla extract
2 teaspoons freshly squeezed lemon juice
1 cup milk, at room temperature
3 egg whites

2 9-inch cake pans

Add salt and baking powder to sifted flour. Sift again and reserve until ready to be used. Place the butter in a mixing bowl and mix it with a wooden spoon until it becomes a bit shiny in appearance. Add the sugar in quarters, stirring well after each addition. When the mixture has become light and most of the granulated quality of the sugar has disappeared, add the beaten egg yolks, which will further dissolve the grainy texture. Continue to stir well and add the vanilla and lemon juice. Stir in ½ cup of the mixed flour and add in ¼ cup of milk, stirring until the batter is smooth. Continue to alternate the flour and milk until the ingredients are used up. (Be sure to end with the flour.) Then beat the whites of eggs to soft peaks and fold them carefully into the batter. Spoon the batter into the two cake pans that have been greased and dusted with flour on the bottom. Be sure that each pan has an equal amount of batter. Set the pans on the middle rack in the center of the oven preheated to 375° and bake for 30 minutes.

Check the cake to see if it has shrunk away from the sides of the pan, or pick the cake pan up and listen for any quiet noises in the cake. If you hear faint sounds, remove from oven and turn the cakes out of the pans onto a wire cake rack. After 10 minutes of cooling, cover the layers with a light, clean cloth until the cakes are ready to be frosted. It is important to cover the cakes in time before they become hard and crusty on the surface.

Boiled White Frosting

A successful boiled white frosting was the desire of every cook. The greatest achievement was to have a crusty outside and a creamy inside. However, when using coconut on top the outside will remain soft.

The most important step in making a good frosting is to see that the syrup spins a definite thread. When a spoon is placed in the boiling syrup and then held up above the pan, the drippings should become a thin thread waving in the air. The eggs should be beaten to firm peaks before the syrup is slowly poured in, then beaten again until the icing stands in peaks and holds the shape it falls in. Then you can add the flavoring and cool a bit before frosting the cake.

> 1 cup plus 2 tablespoons sugar
> ¼ cup cold water
> 3 egg whites (medium to large eggs)
> 1 teaspoon fresh lemon juice
> Coconut (see page 222)

Place the sugar and water in a quart saucepan and leave it for 15 minutes until the water is absorbed. Place the saucepan and contents over a medium-high heat. Watch carefully to keep the syrup from burning around the edges of the pan. Begin beating the egg whites. When the syrup has reached the point where it spins a thread when it falls from the spoon, turn off the heat. Quickly finish beating the egg whites until they hold their shape, then pour the hot syrup slowly into the beaten egg whites. Continue to beat the mixture until the frosting falls in peaks or holds its shape. Add lemon juice or extract. Cool the frosting a few minutes.

Prepare the cake by dusting off any crumbs to prevent them from falling off into the frosting. Place the first layer on a serving plate and spread over with a generous amount of frosting, leaving enough for the top and sides of the cake. Frost the second layer, making sure it is flush with the bottom. Pour the rest of the frosting onto the center of the cake and quickly spread it over the top and around the sides, then sprinkle the grated coconut over the top and sides. A frosted coconut cake is even better when served the next day.

The Coconut

1 medium-sized coconut

It is a good idea to purchase two coconuts just in case one isn't sweet enough. Pick heavy coconuts that sound like they contain a lot of liquid.

Grating the coconut was great fun. After cracking the nut in half with a stout hatchet, catching the water and passing it around for everyone to taste, the meat was pried out with a blunt knife, the brown skin peeled off, and any brown specks were carefully wiped away. The cleaned pieces were grated on the large holes of a four-sided grater and sprinkled over the top and sides of the cake. Press the coconut on lightly with your hand. Be sure and save enough to be sprinkled over in the end to give the cake a fluffy appearance.

Caramel Fudge

2 packed cups brown sugar
2 teaspoons butter
½ cup heavy cream
1 teaspoon vanilla

1 8 x 8 x 2-inch square pan

Mix the brown sugar, butter, and cream together in a saucepan and set on a medium-high burner. Cook to soft-ball stage (230°), stirring continuously until smooth. Add vanilla. Pour into square, buttered pan and set to cool.

Chocolate Fudge

1¼ cups granulated sugar
1 packed cup brown sugar
2 tablespoons melted butter
⅔ cup heavy cream
2 squares Baker's Chocolate, grated fine
2 teaspoons vanilla

1 8 x 8 x 2-inch square pan

In a 2-quart saucepan mix sugar, butter, and cream. Bring to a slow boil, stirring constantly. Continue to boil gently for 5 minutes, add the chocolate, and continue to stir until the mixture thickens. Remove from heat and add the vanilla; pour into buttered pan. Cool before cutting.

Divinity Cream

½ cup clear Karo syrup
2 cups sugar
½ cup cold water
2 egg whites, beaten stiff
1 teaspoon vanilla
1 cup walnut meats

Boil the syrup, sugar, and water together without stirring and when it has thickened test to see if it spins a thread: Place a spoon in the pan of boiling syrup, lift it above the pan, and tilt it so the syrup will quickly run off the spoon—the remainder will fall into a threadlike string when it spins a definite thread. Pour the syrup right away into a bowl of stiff-beaten egg whites. Continue to beat until the mixture becomes thick. When thick, add vanilla and chopped walnut meats or shape into ovals and press half a walnut in top.

Popcorn

Popcorn was magic for us. We enjoyed popping the corn over the fireplace charcoal, watching the grains burst wildly into a mass of snow-white puffballs, and then stirring them into a bowl of melted butter. Sometimes we dipped them into a sugar syrup and made popcorn balls, but the most fun of all was to thread the popped corn onto a lengthy string after it had been dipped into a mixture of powdered sugar, water, and cake coloring. (Our two colors were blue and pink.) Then we would drape the string around the Christmas tree, making a beautiful decoration with candles nesting in tufts of cotton scattered around the tree. Of course, the candles were never lit.

Sugared Popcorn

FOR STRINGING
1½ cups sugar
1 cup water
1 teaspoon salt
Cake coloring
2 quarts freshly popped corn

1 3-quart saucepan

Cook the sugar, water, and salt until the syrup forms a soft ball when dropped into cold water. Remove from the fire and add 2 or 3 drops of cake coloring. Beat with a spoon until it becomes slightly creamy. Drop in the popcorn and stir quickly until each kernel is coated with sugar. Put on a platter and separate the grains of corn. If you desire to use a second color, repeat the process, using a few drops of pink or other coloring in the sugar syrup.

Bowl of Nuts and Oranges and Raisins

The bowl of oranges, nuts, and raisin clusters was Christmas. There was no other time of the year that the house had that particular aroma. It seemed as if the warmth of the hearth fire extracted the aromatic oils from the delicious Valencia oranges filling the house, mingling with the fragrance of pine needles, juniper berries, and holiday baking. We did enjoy the locally grown chestnuts, hazelnuts, and black walnuts, but the imported ones had more charm because they came only at Christmas from faraway Valencia, Jordan, and Brazil.

The bowl was set upon one end of the mantelpiece for all to see and enjoy. In the evening, while sitting before the fire, we would enjoy tasting the rich, meaty Brazil nuts that were bursting with oil when we chewed them. We were all fascinated with the crisp paper shells of Jordan almonds and their almost bittersweet flavor. There was nothing like the plump, chewy dried raisins, with a sweet flavor mingling with nuts—flavors we experienced only at Christmas. It is hard to describe the taste of those oranges; their sweetness had no equal as we ate them. Mother would gather up all the orange peels and dry them for flavoring sauces for summer puddings. She also used them to flavor tea. The fire would be snapping and crackling as if it, too, knew it was holiday time.

I can't remember Mother cautioning us not to overeat, but I do remember her telling us a story of a very hungry man who passed by a farmhouse while the farm wife was making pies and asked for one. She began to taste them to see which one was the best and ended up eating them all, whereupon she turned into a woodpecker. When you see woodpecker, notice its front. That is the pie lady, still wearing her white apron.

For recipe for **Blackberry Wine,** see page 100.

LATE WINTER

The New Year ushered in long and continued cold weather, the kind needed for developing thick ice on the ponds and rivers. When it reached the desired thickness, the men of Freetown would go out and help cut it into 3- to 4-foot pieces, about 2 to 3 feet thick, and then haul it in. The icehouse was a deep, round cellar about 20 to 30 feet deep, with a roof and door, lined with poles and filled with a good layer of straw with a strong ladder extending down into it. The ice was placed in this cellar and covered with more straw. Once filled, it was left alone until needed on hot summer days. Most farmers had their own icehouses, but we got ours from the icehouse at Lahore. We used it for making ice cream, lemonade, cooling the milk, and sometimes drinking water. It was a great treat to bring the ice home in a burlap bag, chipping off small pieces to eat on a hot day. After the icehouse was all filled up, most activity ceased except for morning and evening feeding, milking, and bringing in water and firewood.

It was in between these daily chores that the people of Freetown found more time for visiting each other. There were visitors from nearby communities, especially to visit with Grandpa. A person of his age group (80 years and older) would arrive on horseback or in a buggy, unbridle his horse, and put it in the barn with ours. Then he would visit us for a week or two or three. We liked having visitors. It gave the house a festive air and neighbors would drop by to greet the guest. We children were able to be alone in the next room and relax our behavior without being noticed. A great fire would be going in the fireplace, and we would serve homemade cake and homemade wines that seemed to have been made for just such occasions. There would be lively conversations, with the aged men doing most of the talking and the young adults of my father's age group listening. I would be listening, too, hanging between my father's knees and watching the logs burning in the fireplace and bugs desperately trying to escape from the burning logs with only me being aware of their desperate plight. I was too young then to understand why so much time was spent in discussion. It was only afterward that I realized they were still awed by the experience of chattel slavery fifty years ago, and of having become freedmen. It was something that they never tired of talking about. It gave birth to a song I often heard them sing, "My Soul Look Back and Wonder How I Got Over."

While the very intense discussion went on inside, snow blanketed the earth outside. The mood was right for a pot of stew cooking on the side of the fireplace, and some ash cakes, which were made of fresh-ground cornmeal, salt, and water—just enough to make a fairly stiff dough. The cakes were then molded by hand into an 8 x 4-inch egg-shaped pone, wrapped in cabbage leaves, or left unwrapped and put into a clean bed of ashes in the fireplace and left to cook until needed. The summer kitchen had been closed and most of the cooking was done now in the fire hearth.

The main meal was served in the evening because of the short daylight hours of winter and the early feeding of the stock. This was the time to draw upon the canned vegetables and fruits that had been prepared during those unbearable hot days of the past summer. In addition, there was sausage, liver pudding, spareribs, wild game from the hunting parties, and wild watercress. No winter meal was complete without a fat, old Barred rock hen saved for a cold day, stewed and served piping hot with dumplings made of a rich biscuit dough. The most popular fresh vegetable was the wild watercress that was gathered from the lowlands just before or after a snow. This was said to be a fine source of iron, good to eat during the dark, gray days of winter, served with baked tomatoes, boiled shoulder, and mashed potatoes. We also had thick soups of home-grown dried beans with slices of pork and hot, crusty breads. And for dessert there would be bread puddings, deep-dish pies, and compotes of canned fruit.

Aside from entertaining, there was a great interest in the new seed catalogues that began to arrive after the first of the year. The highly colored pages of seed catalogues were very tempting, although for the most part we used our own seed year after year. (They were not hybrid in those days.) My mother would often be tempted to buy new kinds of vegetables. The seeds were easy to grow and as soon as something was ready to pick we had to cook it and see what that new vegetable tasted like.

The winter vegetables would consist of some root crops that could be left in the ground all winter and gathered as needed, such as turnips, parsnips, tube artichokes, and salsify with its flavor of oyster bisque—a refreshing change from potatoes in late winter—cabbage, canned corn, and beans. No canned fruit had the fragrance of canned pears. Canned blackberries and peaches were also favorites of ours. So was canned applesauce made into two-crust pies. And a treat was a bowl of clean snow flavored with vanilla and with sweetened heavy cream folded into it, which we called Snow Cream. There were also the perennial dried apples for making dried apple pie, and dried peaches to chew on.

Winter must have seemed forever for our mother, a lover of the outdoors. Along in February she would save all of the eggshells, line them up on the windowsill, place the seed of a green bean in each one, and add about a tablespoon of water. When sprouted enough she would set them, still in the shells, into a prepared row and cover them with soil on the first warm day of spring.

Winter was surely behind us by St. Patrick's Day. That was the day when we planted our white potatoes. The people of Freetown always made a lazy bed and it is still done this way today. This is how it went: First we would cut off pieces of potatoes that had a bud or eye in them, until there were enough to set out on top of a 25-foot squared-off patch of unploughed, clean ground—perhaps a half a bushel of eyes. The pieces would be put into a tub and sprinkled with a bit of lime to keep them from rotting on the cut surface. The eyes were set out by us because we were small and didn't have to suffer from bending over. Then we would cover them over with about two feet of wheat straw and leave them alone to grow up through it, bloom, and die down. When all the foliage had turned brown and was well dried—late in July—the straw was raked off. At that point there would be what looked like a great group of hens' nests filled with large, rounded eggs. All that was left for us to do was to pick up the potatoes and store them in a cool, shady place for later use. If left in the sun they would turn green and become bitter. I forgot to mention that the pieces left over from the eyes were used for cooking, as they were our own seed and untreated. We would have potatoes in every imaginable way until we couldn't stand them anymore.

A SNOWY WINTER BREAKFAST

Beef Kidney Pie in Puff Pastry

Oven-Cooked Ham Slices

Hard-Boiled Eggs

Country Toast

Damson Preserves

Stewed Quince

Coffee

Cocoa

On a cold, snowy Sunday morning we often enjoyed a breakfast of kidney pie with hard-boiled eggs, oven-fried ham, country-style toast, damson preserves, coffee, and cocoa for the children, with a side dish of canned, stewed quince.

Beef Kidney Pie in Puff Pastry

Kidney stew was considered an extra dish served only for Sunday breakfast, Sunday being a leisurely day. All the regular chores were laid aside, except for feeding, milking, and bringing in wood. Sunday was the day we had fresh-made yeast bread and dishes such as smothered beefsteak, fried chicken, stew, and delectable accompaniments to go with them.

Whenever the local miller killed a beef cow he gave the organs away. Sometimes we would also get a sheep's head from him, or a veal head, and most of the time a kidney. I remember the kidney stew cooking on the back of the wood cookstove and later spooned into a pastry-lined baking pan and baked in the oven.

Sunday breakfasts were memorable ones. While inhaling the aromas from the kitchen, my father and later my uncle would gather us around the fire and we would have a great time singing and reciting poetry until breakfast was ready.

PUFF PASTRY   *Serves 4 to 5*
2 cups flour
½ teaspoon salt
½ cup cold water
1 cup (½ pound) chilled butter

FILLING
10 small, white onions
2 beef kidneys
2 tablespoons flour
½ cup (1 stick) butter
¼ cup sherry (optional)
2 medium-sized onions, finely chopped or grated
Pinch of thyme
1 small bay leaf
3 medium-sized white potatoes, cut in quarters
1 teaspoon sugar
Salt
½ teaspoon fresh-ground black pepper
¼ cup finely cut parsley

First prepare the pastry. Sift the flour and salt into a mixing bowl. Stir in a generous ½ cup of cold water and mix the dough well by hand. Let it rest on the table for 15 minutes. Then place the dough on a lightly floured surface and roll it out, turning the dough as you roll to achieve an even thickness. For kidney pie it's better not rolled too thin—about ¼ inch thick or a bit less. Roll the dough out on a floured board into a rectangle about 9 x 18 inches. If the butter is in ¼-pound pieces, slice each lengthwise 4 times, so that you have 8 strips. Place the pieces close together on one half of the pastry. Fold it over and seal the edges by rolling the rolling pin over them. Turn and press lightly with the rolling pin to spread the butter. Roll the dough mixture into a long strip, being careful not to break a hole in the pastry. Roll gently and carefully, keeping your rolling pin and board lightly floured. After rolling the dough into a long strip, fold it in half and then again in half. Roll out again. After repeating this process three times, leave the dough to rest in the refrigerator until needed. When ready to use divide the dough in two for lining and covering the casserole.

Prepare the small, white onions by peeling off the outer skin and piercing the bottom of each onion with the pointed end of the knife, making a cross (+). The incision on the bottom will prevent the center from slipping out of the onion while cooking. Set aside. Prepare the kidneys by first removing the thin skin covering them. Wash the kidneys well in cold water, wipe dry, and cut into 1½-inch pieces. Sprinkle them over with flour. Heat a skillet and add ⅓ of the butter. When it foams add the chopped or grated onion and brown well without burning. Add the kidney pieces and sear well. Add sherry. Spoon the contents of the skillet into a 2-quart saucepan. Add the thyme, bay leaf, and pour in just enough heated water to cover. Set over a medium-high burner to simmer gently for 45 minutes. After 30 minutes of cooking add the white potatoes.

While the stew is cooking heat a skillet and add the rest of the butter and a teaspoon of sugar to help the white onions brown nicely. When foaming stage is reached add the onions. Brown by keeping the fire rather brisk and shaking the pan continuously for about 10 minutes. Remove the onions from the pan and hold aside until the kidneys are cooked. Season the kidneys to taste with salt and pepper. Add parsley. Line a fireproof casserole with the puff pastry and spoon in the kidney mixture, then add the browned onions. Moisten the edges of the bottom crust and unroll the top crust over the casserole. Pierce the top of the pie well to release the steam. Bake in a preheated 425° oven for 1 hour and 15 minutes. Remove from the oven and let rest a few minutes before serving.

For recipe for **Oven-Cooked Ham Slices,** see page 19.

Hard-Boiled Eggs

Have a non-aluminum saucepan of water boiling—not aluminum because the eggs will turn it dark. Some say a teaspoon of salt in the water will prevent the shells from cracking. Have 4 to 8 eggs at room temperature and lower each egg into the boiling water. Then turn the heat down and allow the eggs to just barely simmer. After 15 minutes of cooking plunge the eggs into cold water for a minute. Remove from the cold water and serve in the shell.

Country Toast

We did consider oven-toasted bread special if biscuits were short and there wasn't time to make more. We would slice some bread from our homemade loaf, butter it liberally, and place it in the oven. When cooked it would be browned in the areas where there was no butter and the buttered part would be golden and soft. This was the most delicious way of toasting bread. It can be done under the broiler as well, especially if the bread is placed on a hot broiler pan. That will crisp the underside of the bread and the top will be brown and crisp in spots where there is no butter. The combination of crispy brown and soft buttered bread is simply heavenly.

For recipe for **Damson Preserves,** see page 157.

Stewed Quince

Quince is a highly fragrant and delicious Old World fruit, once a part of every homestead in the South. We always put them up in the fall because they kept well and gave us the good flavor of tart fruit in the winter. It is still appreciated by those who remember it. It can often be found in city markets through October.

2 large quince
Water to cover fruit
1¼ cups sugar

Serves 4 to 5

Select sound quince when they appear in the market. They can be kept until they turn yellow and highly fragrant. At this point they should be cooked. Wash, cut in half, core, and slice into quarters with skin on. Cook gently with cold water just covering the fruit for 30 minutes, until tender. Add in the sugar and continue cooking for another 15 minutes. The compote can be served warm as well as cold.

A DUCK DINNER IN WINTER

Braised Muscovy Duck in Natural Sauce

Buttered Green Beans

Fried Eggplant or Purée of Chestnuts

Applesauce with Nutmeg

Slices of Yeast Bread

Butter

Lemon Meringue Pie

Coffee

The Muscovy was a large breed of ducks raised in our area and they were a part of every barnyard fowl family. After watching the mother duck line up her little brood of fluffy yellow ducklings and take them down to the stream below the barn for their first swimming lessons, we always hated to consume them. We would wait until winter before picking out an older duck for cooking. It was usually served as a change from fresh pork and holiday meats with chestnuts from the grove and applesauce we had put up and sometimes for dessert a fragile lemon pie with the most tender crust.

Braised Muscovy Duck in Natural Sauce

Mother had a great way of cooking a duck with the help of the wood cookstove. Some believed that the oak wood helped to flavor food. After the duck was dressed it was hung in the meat house for at least a week. Then she would prepare it by wiping it inside and out with a damp cloth, and rubbing it over with a paste of soft butter, salt, pepper, and paprika before baking.

> ¼ cup soft butter　　　　　　　　　　*Serves 5 to 6*
> 2 teaspoons salt
> ½ teaspoon black pepper
> 2 teaspoons paprika
> 1 8-pound duck
> 2 medium-large onions, sliced

Mix the butter, salt, pepper, and paprika well together into a paste and rub it over the duck. Place duck into an open roasting pan about the size of the duck with slices of onion all around and a bit of water added. Bake for 2 hours or more at 350°. When cooked, remove the duck to a hot platter and skim the fat from the juices. This natural sauce was served in a separate bowl, and we loved to dunk our bread into it.

For recipe for **Buttered Green Beans,** see page 59.

Fried Eggplant

Eggplant was another dish served in winter, sometimes for breakfast as well as dinner. They held over until winter in our area of Virginia. Mother would peel and slice them after supper, then place a plate over them and set a heavy flatiron on the plate to press out the liquid. The next morning she would remove the cover, wipe the slices dry, and dip each slice in flour. She then dipped the floured slices into a mixture of egg and milk.

> 1 medium eggplant   *Serves 5 to 6*
> ⅓ cup milk
> 3 eggs
> 1 teaspoon salt
> 1 cup flour
> 1 cup fine bread crumbs
> ½ cup (1 stick) butter, lard, or oil

Peel and slice eggplant into ½-inch-thick slices. Sprinkle lightly with salt. Press with a heavy weight for an hour or more. Pat dry.

Combine milk, eggs, and salt. Dip each slice first into the flour, then into the egg mixture, and then into the bread crumbs. Treat both sides this way and fry in hot fat, lard, butter, or oil. Cook on each side for about 2½ minutes. Eggplant should be a golden-brown color. Serve hot.

Purée of Chestnuts

One of my grandfathers had a small grove of chestnut trees. That is how we first came to know about chestnuts. He would bring them in the fall in a burlap bag and we would have great fun cooking them in the fireplace ashes, or sometimes we would boil them. Later, unfortunately, the trees became blighted and the grove died out. Now in the city when I walk down the street in the fall and see the chestnuts coming into the market, I always get a feeling of home and remember our fireplace.

Chestnuts are a bit troublesome to prepare, but are worth the effort in goodness. First, cut a slit in the chestnuts on the flat side. Place them into a pie pan and set in a hot oven for 10 to 15 minutes. Remove from the oven. Peel off the shell and the skin while still warm. When peeled, put them into boiling water to cover and cook gently for an hour or until tender. Remove from the water, drain, mash, and add a pinch of salt and ⅓ cup of hot, rich milk. Mix well and press the chestnuts through a potato ricer. Leave the chestnuts the way they fall into the bowl and serve as is.

Applesauce with Nutmeg

Applesauce was forever popular. Using the first apples of the season, even before they were ripe, made an interestingly flavored sauce.

5 medium-sized apples   *Serves 5 to 6*
Pinch of salt
⅓ cup sugar
Freshly grated nutmeg

Pare the apples. Cut in half, quarter, core, and place them into a saucepan. Sprinkle over the prepared apples a pinch of salt and the sugar. Cover and cook over a medium burner. After 10 minutes of cooking remove the cover. Enough water should have developed to cook the apples. Shake the saucepan around to stir the apples. Leave uncovered and continue cooking gently until all the juice has dried down and the sauce is thick. Remove from the burner and flavor with fresh-grated nutmeg to taste.

For recipe for **Yeast Bread,** see page 73.

Lemon Meringue Pie

Lemon meringue pie, like white frosting, was considered a great achievement; every cook tried to excel in the art. Mother made the most fragile lemon pie. Her filling was very delicately jelled in a crispy, thin crust with a ½-inch-thick meringue that almost floated upon the unstable transparent filling. It was indeed a delight to look at as well as to eat. She would make lemon pie as a treat for us after we had finished a good job of weeding the cornfield or when for some reason she wanted to make us happy. The filling was stirred right on the stove without a double boiler, until it became transparent. Then it was set to cool while Mother made the crust. Her crusts were made with home-rendered lard and they never failed, but that is hard to come by in city markets today. And her meringue she simply beat with a dinner fork on a large meat platter and then spooned it into an island upon the filling.

I have tried to reconstruct the ingredients she used for the recipe given.

CRUST
⅔ cup sifted, unbleached, all-purpose flour
¼ teaspoon salt
5 tablespoons cold, unsalted butter (or good
    lard), cut into small pieces
3 tablespoons water

1 8 or 9-inch pie plate

Sift the flour and salt together into a mixing bowl. Add the butter and blend quickly with your fingertips or with a pastry blender. Sprinkle in the water and blend the dough together lightly. Put the dough onto a lightly floured surface to rest for about 15 minutes. Roll out lightly to fill a 9-inch pie pan. Roll the crust upon the rolling pin and unroll it over the pie plate. This is the best way to handle a short crust. Trim the edges and prick the crust's bottom with a dinner fork. Set this into a preheated 400° oven to bake from 12 to 15 minutes. Halfway through, look at the crust. If it has puffed spots over it just pierce them lightly with the fork. They will deflate. Continue to bake until the crust is lightly browned. Remove from the oven and set upon a wire rack to cool. When the crust is cold, fill it with the lemon filling.

> FILLING
> 1 cup sugar
> ¼ teaspoon salt
> ¼ cup hot water
> ½ cup lemon juice, strained through a fine
>   strainer
> 1 tablespoon butter
> 5 egg yolks, beaten

Put the sugar, salt, water, and lemon juice into a 2-quart, non-aluminum saucepan, and set over a medium burner, stirring until the sugar is completely dissolved. Then add the butter. Have the beaten yolks in a bowl. Pour some of the hot mixture into the yolks, stirring the yolks as you pour to prevent curdling. Then pour the yolk mixture back into the saucepan. Return the pan to the stove and cook carefully, stirring continuously until the contents become transparent and definitely coat the spoon. Set the filling out to cool.

> MERINGUE TOPPING
> 2 egg whites
> 3 tablespoons sugar
> 1 teaspoon vanilla

Put the egg whites on a platter and beat them with a wire whisk or a fork. Beat until foamy. Add sugar and continue to beat until whites hold in stiff peaks. Add the vanilla and spoon the meringue onto the filling. Spread it in the desired design and set into a preheated 325° oven. Bake until lightly browned, about 15 minutes.

A WINTER DINNER

Beef à la Mode
Salad of Wild Watercress with Vinegar and Oil
Crusty Bread
Butter
Deep-Dish Apple Pie with Nutmeg Sauce
Coffee

In early winter we would get a quarter of beef in the hide and hang it, using pieces of it during the coldest months. Beef à la mode was a special-occasion dish served hot with lots of sauce, our own canned green beans, and a dessert of deep-dish apple pie with nutmeg.

Beef à la Mode

Beef à la mode is another name that is familiar to our area along with blanc mange, divinity, and Lahore. It has no equal when made with the local butchered beef and loads of home-grown onions. A delicious dish served hot on a cold winter day and equally good served cold on a hot summer day.

4 pounds chuck, or bottom round   *Serves 6 to 8*
3 tablespoons butter
Larding fat
Salt and pepper
4 pounds yellow onions, sliced
Bouquet of parsley, thyme, and bay leaf
½ calf's foot cut into 3 or 4 pieces
2 cups claret
1 cup beef bouillon
1 rounded tablespoon brown sugar
3 carrots, sliced
2 teaspoons granulated sugar
1 dozen small, white onions

Prepare the beef by having the butcher lard it, or lard it at home yourself. Take the strips of larding fat sprinkled with salt and pepper and put them into a needle, larding the meat throughout. Tie it well and sear on all sides in 1 tablespoon of foaming butter. Searing will help to seal in the juices during the long cooking time. After removing the meat from the skillet, add the sliced onions and sauté until slightly brown. Put the browned onions in the bottom of the cooking pot. Add the bouquet of spices, the beef, and the pieces of calf's foot. Heat the claret. When hot but not boiling, set aflame, hold above the burner and tilt back and forth until all of the alcohol has been burned off. Add the cup of beef bouillon to the wine and brown sugar, stir well, and pour over the beef and contents of the pot. (The liquid should cover about two thirds of the meat.) Cover with a tight lid and set the pot into the center of a preheated 225° oven. Leave to cook for 4 hours, turning the meat halfway through the cooking. As the meat cooks the temperature may have to be reduced. The contents in the pot should simmer very slowly.

An hour before the beef à la mode is finished, slice the carrots, sauté them in 1 tablespoon butter, and add them to the beef. Wipe the skillet out and add another tablespoon of butter and 2 teaspoons of granulated sugar. Heat until foaming, add the white onions, and shake the pan around until the onions are well-coated and nicely browned. Add to the pot. When the cooking is finished, place the meat on a platter. Set the onions and carrots around it. Remove the pieces of calf's foot, cube them, and add to the meat platter. Press the rest of the sliced onions and sauce into a bowl through a sieve, skimming off all fat, and heat the sauce until it is very hot. Pour over the meat platter and serve immediately, piping hot.

For recipe for **Crusty Yeast Bread,** see page 46.

Salad of Wild Watercress

Wild watercress grew abundantly around the spring and in low, moist spots, so it was almost always available for garnishing, for cooking, and for salad. Wild cress is very peppery, so you might be surprised biting into it for the first time. The flavor is somewhat tamed when served on a plate along with any heavy-flavored meat.

3 tablespoons cider vinegar   *Serves 4 to 5*
4 tablespoons olive oil
½ teaspoon salt
½ teaspoon dry mustard
½ teaspoon fresh-grated black pepper
A bowl of tender cress leaves

Place the vinegar, oil, salt, mustard, and pepper into a glass bottle and shake well. When the cress has been washed and dried and is ready to be served, shake the dressing again and sprinkle it over the bowl of cress.

Deep-Dish Apple Pie with Nutmeg Sauce

1 recipe pie pastry (page 217)   *Serves 4 to 5*
7 large apples (about 3 pounds), Cortland,
    McIntosh, or any tart apple of good flavor
1 teaspoon freshly ground nutmeg
⅔ cup sugar
5 thin pats chilled butter

1 8 x 8 x 2-inch Pyrex baking dish

Preheat oven to 450°. Remove pie pastry from refrigerator for about 15 to 20 minutes before rolling it out, so that it will be easy to handle. Divide in half, and roll out the bottom crust into a 10-inch square, then roll it onto the pin and carefully unroll it over the baking dish. Gently shape it into the bottom and sides of the dish.

Peel the apples, quarter, core, and seed them, and slice each quarter into 4 slices. Place the apple wedges in layers in the pan, and when half full, sprinkle with the nutmeg and half the sugar. Fill the pan with almost all the apples until they are level with the top, and then place remaining apple slices in a mound in the center. Dot the apples with the pats of butter and add the remaining sugar.

Roll out the top crust and unroll it off the rolling pin over the apples. Firm it down gently with your fingers and trim off any edges.

Make vents all over the top crust with a pointed knife, but not closer than 2 inches from the edge, or the juices will run out and over the edge of the pan.

Place the pie in the middle rack of the preheated oven for 10 minutes, then lower the heat to 425° and bake an additional 40 minutes. Let cool for a half hour and serve with nutmeg sauce (see page 142).

A BEAN SUPPER

Kidney Bean Soup

or

Baked Beans

Salsify

Crackling Bread

Jelly Roll

Coffee

My mother often served us a supper of kidney bean soup or a pot of baked beans on a winter night with crackling bread, buttered salsify, and the famous cake of that time, jelly roll, filled with one of the tart, homemade jellies from summer canning. Stews and thick soups cooked leisurely in the side of the hearth and were enjoyed before a lively fire that sent up loud reports of snaps and crackles as if it knew we were enjoying our meal after a day of ploughing through the snow to feed the stock and gather in the evening wood.

Kidney Bean Soup

1 pound kidney beans   *Serves 4 to 5*
1 pound smoked shoulder of pork
⅛ teaspoon fresh or dried thyme
Salt and freshly ground pepper

Pick the beans over, wash well, and set to soak overnight with water to cover. The next morning, place the beans in a 3-quart pot. Add the meat and thyme. Pour in enough water to cover about 2 inches from the top of the pot. Set over a medium-high burner. When signs of boiling begin, turn the burner very low and leave to simmer very slowly for 7 to 8 hours. When the broth becomes rather syrupy, season with salt and pepper to taste. This is a dish that can be cooked ahead and reheated.

Baked Beans

Beans were grown mostly to be eaten during summer while in their green state and many of these were canned for use in winter, as I've described in the Summer chapter. As well, we always planted a few late varieties for drying, such as red kidney and a type of navy bean. They were perfect for simmering on the back of the stove or on a fire-hearth overnight. We did not really bake them but put them through a long, slow process of heating, and they always remained firm with a thick cream sauce. We didn't use any sugar—we would just add an onion the size of a medium egg and with that and the long cooking the beans developed a sweetness of their own.

Field and garden vegetable seeds were not hybrid and could be planted year after year in the same general area, being nourished by the dead foliage of the last beans, enriched by well-rotted barnyard manure, and grown on their own steam without the aid of fertilizer as a booster to hurry them up.

1 pound pea beans or navy beans
4 cups bottled water
1 medium onion, finely chopped
½ pound streaky lean salt pork
½ teaspoon dry mustard
2 tablespoons tomato purée

*Serves 4 to 5,
with leftovers*

1 3-quart iron pot

Pick over and wash the beans, first in warm water to loosen any dirt sticking to them, then rinse in cold water. Set them to soak overnight in a big saucepan with enough water to just barely cover them. In the morning drain away the water and add 4 cups fresh, cold bottled water (or fresh spring water, if you have it) and set the beans to simmer gently for 15 minutes. Then take the iron pot and place the finely chopped onion in the bottom. Rinse the streak of lean off and leaving the rind on, score it, and add it to the pot. Then add the beans, along with the water they simmered in, the dry mustard, and the tomato purée, stirring well. Cover, set into a preheated 250° oven, and cook at that temperature for 6 hours or longer. During the cooking keep the water level even with the beans but not covering them. Have a kettle of hot water handy so as not to slow down the cooking when you have to add some. An hour before the cooking is finished, uncover the beans, but keep adding the water if necessary up to ½ hour before removing them. They are delicious served with a green salad, crusty yeast bread, and sweet butter. They can also be cooked ahead and reheated.

For recipe for **Salsify,** see page 38.

Cracklings

Cracklings are the crispy bits strained from pork fat after it is rendered. The fat is usually from the loin, and it can be found cut in strips in the large supermarkets and butcher shops throughout the year (2 pounds will yield 2 cups of cracklings). To prepare the fat for rendering, cut away any lean bits or skin because they will become hard and spoil your cracklings. Wipe each piece off in case there is any residue left from the butcher's block. Cut the fat into ½-inch pieces. Cook in a heavy-bottomed saucepan or iron skillet with ¼ cup of water to avoid the fat sticking in the beginning. Start on medium heat, watch closely, and stir often at first until the fat begins to melt. Lower the heat and let the fat separate slowly. The pieces of fat will begin to float. The defatted, browned pieces will go to the bottom and shrink to half their original size. Strain the fat away; it is excellent lard for making bread and frying. Leave the defatted pieces to cool. When ready to use, cut into ¼-inch pieces.

Crackling Bread

2 cups water-ground white cornmeal   *Serves 4 to 5*
½ teaspoon salt
½ teaspoon baking soda
½ teaspoon Royal Baking Powder
1 cup cracklings, cut in ¼-inch pieces
2 tablespoons butter
1 cup buttermilk

1 9 x 10-inch baking pan

Sift together meal, salt, soda, and baking powder into a mixing bowl. Sprinkle the cracklings over the meal mixture and stir well. Put the butter into a baking pan, about 9 x 10 inches, and set it in the oven.

Pour the buttermilk into the meal mixture, stirring vigorously. This is a stiffer dough than other meal batters. Remove the pan from the oven, tilting it back and forth to butter the whole surface. Pour the excess butter into the meal batter and return the pan to the oven to keep it hot while you finish stirring the batter. Remove the pan from the oven and spoon in the meal batter, spreading it evenly over the pan with the back of the spoon. Bake for 25 to 30 minutes at 400°. Cut into squares and serve hot. It's deliciously chewy and crusty.

Jelly Roll

Soft butter
4 eggs
2 teaspoons cold water
¾ cup sugar, heated for 5 minutes in medium
   oven
2 teaspoons vanilla
¾ cup sifted flour
½ cup currant jelly
Powdered sugar

*Serves 4 to 5
with leftovers*

1 10 x 15-inch jelly-roll pan

Butter the jelly-roll pan. Line it with wax paper, which should be buttered on both sides. Heat a mixing bowl by pouring boiling water into it. Empty and wipe dry. Mix the eggs, water, and heated sugar. Beat at high speed until the eggs become light and rise high in the bowl (12 to 15 minutes). Add the vanilla and beat for a second. Remove the beater and start sifting the flour in bit by bit, folding gently and thoroughly after each sifting. When all the flour has been added, spoon the batter onto the jelly-roll pan. Spread the batter into all four corners. Set into a preheated 400° oven for about 15 minutes. When done, turn out onto a sheet of wax paper, remove the pan, and leave to cool. Then peel off the wax paper, and cut away any edges that may be crusty so the roll will be smooth. Spread over with currant jelly and roll up by catching the two ends facing you and rolling them forward. When completed, lightly dust with powdered sugar.

A WINTER DINNER

Chicken with Dumplings

Glazed Carrots

Crusty Yeast Bread

Butter

Warm Gingerbread with Sweetened Whipped Cream

Coffee

Chicken with dumplings of biscuit dough and a dessert of warm gingerbread was another cold winter day's meal we enjoyed after a day of trudging through the snow.

Chicken with Dumplings

½ cup (1 stick) butter
1 large fowl (about 4 pounds), cut up
3 or 4 chicken wings
1 onion, finely grated
Stock or water to cover
2 stalks celery with leaves
6 peppercorns
Salt and freshly ground pepper

DUMPLINGS
2 cups sifted flour
¼ teaspoon salt
2 rounded teaspoons Royal Baking Powder
1 teaspoon brown sugar
2 tablespoons butter
⅔ cup milk

Heat a large iron pot and add the butter. When sizzling, add the pieces of fowl and the extra wings. Sprinkle in the grated onion and stir and turn the mixture, being careful not to let it stick or brown. When each piece is seared, pour in enough stock or water just to cover the pieces of chicken in the pot. The extra chicken wings will add thickness to the broth; the second joint and the tip contain a gelatine substance which will give body to the dish. Next add the celery stalks and peppercorns. Cover the pot and allow the mixture to simmer slowly for about 2 hours until the chicken is done, which will depend upon the age of the fowl or hen. (Test a wing to see if it is tender.)

While the chicken is cooking prepare the dumplings.

Sift flour, salt, baking powder, and sugar into a mixing bowl. Add the butter, blending with fingertips. Add the milk and mix well. Spoon the dough onto a floured surface and roll it out evenly ¼ inch in diameter. Cut into 1-inch rounds or diamond shapes.

When chicken is cooked, remove the pieces and keep warm. Strain the stock, discarding the peppercorns, celery stalks, and bits of onion. Return the broth to the pot. Season with salt to taste and a good grating of freshly ground pepper. Add in the dumplings. Cover and cook for 20 minutes.

Pour the sauce and dumplings over the warm chicken and serve.

Glazed Carrots

Carrots were not among the earliest root vegetables planted in Free-town, but Mother was always interested in trying new seed. I re-member the neighbors coming to look at the carrots when they were dug. We cooked them and decided they were liked served creamed, as many of the vegetables were then. Today, carrots are not as sweet as they were then and a good way to preserve some of their flavor is to sauté them.

4 to 5 medium-sized carrots   *Serves 4 to 5*
2 tablespoons butter
2 tablespoons cold water
½ teaspoon salt
2 teaspoons sugar

Scrape, wash, and dry the carrots with a clean cloth and slice in thin, round slices about as thick as a nickel. Heat a heavy skillet and add the butter. When it foams and becomes very hot, but not burn-ing, spill in the carrot slices, stirring constantly for a few minutes. Sprinkle the cold water over the carrots and cover tightly. Turn the heat down to keep the contents from browning, yet high enough to continue cooking. After 4 minutes remove the cover, stir the carrots, and test for tenderness. If tender enough, sprinkle over the salt and sugar. Turn up the burner and stir briskly to melt the sugar without browning. Serve hot.

For recipe for **Crusty Yeast Bread,** see page 46.

Warm Gingerbread with Sweetened Whipped Cream

Warm gingerbread was uppermost in our minds when the sorghum cane began to ripen, because sorghum molasses was such an important ingredient in gingerbread. Sorghum is a plant that looks very much like corn, with the exception of the grain which is formed in the tassel. (In Africa, land of its origin, the grain is used for flour.) Most farmers grew a small patch of sorghum. It was harvested in the fall, tassel and leaves removed. The cane was put into a mill driven by two horses moving in a circle, clockwise, pressing out the juice as they walked around. When it was all pressed out it was poured into a large vat and cooked to a heavy, sugary syrup known as sorghum molasses.

The aroma of the new crop filled the kitchen. There would be molasses for breakfast and gingerbread galore until the novelty wore off. I remember Mother dipping a teacup into the stone crock of molasses and spooning out the sugary syrup into the pungent ginger batter. Warm gingerbread with fresh, skimmed, heavy cream was an exotic treat after a meal of fresh pork or game on a chilly fall evening.

Sorghum molasses has disappeared from the cupboard today but can be found in certain shops around most cities.

2 cups flour
¼ teaspoon baking soda
2 teaspoons Royal Baking Powder
½ teaspoon ground cloves
1 tablespoon powdered ginger
1 teaspoon cinnamon
½ teaspoon salt
½ cup butter (1 stick) and ¼ cup lard mixed together
1 cup hot water
2 eggs, beaten
1½ cups sorghum molasses

1 8 x 8 x 2-inch baking pan

WHIPPED CREAM
1 cup heavy chilled cream
2 teaspoons vanilla
2 tablespoons sugar

In a large mixing bowl sift flour, soda, baking powder, cloves, ginger, cinnamon, and salt. Mix the lard and butter in the hot water and when melted pour into the flour mixture. Stir well, then add beaten eggs. Continue stirring, add molasses, and stir well again. Spoon the batter into the buttered and floured baking pan. Set to bake in a preheated 350° oven for 35 to 40 minutes. Whip the chilled cream until it forms soft peaks but is not too stiff, then add sugar and vanilla. Serve with warm gingerbread.

APPENDIX & INDEX

A Note on Baking Powder

I have discovered recently that Royal Baking Powder, which I call for throughout the book, is no longer being made because of the rising cost of cream of tartar. I would hope that the fact that it will no longer be available will stimulate an interest in searching for other forms of leavening. For my tastes, double-acting baking powder—the only kind you'll be able to buy now—contains so many chemicals that it gives a bitter aftertaste to baked goods, and even more so if the product is held over a day or so.

The women of Freetown used to make lovely cakes and breads that rose by the power of beaten egg whites, which were folded in at the last minute. For biscuits and corn breads they relied upon sour milk and baking soda as the raising agent, and, of course, yeast can be utilized in many types of cakes as well as breads. If cream of tartar is available, good results can be achieved by mixing 2 parts cream of tartar with 1 part baking soda, and using this in place of baking powder in the same amount the recipe calls for.

A Note on Herbs to Grow on the Windowsill

PERENNIALS	ANNUALS
Tarragon	Chervil
Thyme	Arugula
Chives	Garlic

Many herbs grew uncultivated in the corners and along the sides of our garden: sage, horseradish, black basil, thyme, chervil, peppermint, and horehound. The food had so much flavor of its own, herbs were used in a very subtle manner. But we did use them, not only for special occasions but for simple, everyday cooking. Tarragon for all types of mayonnaise sauces. Chervil as a natural for sweet green peas, beans, salads, and sauces. Picked dried sage was indispensable at hog-butchering. For a more subtle flavor of garlic, use the green sprouts instead of the clove bulb— it sprouts readily in a warm room. Thyme was as usual for soups, stews, and stuffings; chives for sauces, salads, and omelets.

They all grow really well on the sill of an east window. Planted in good soil from a nursery, chervil can be planted in succession every other week. The seeds sprout readily. Plant 5 or 6 seeds in a 4-inch flowerpot. They grow well and last a few weeks. All plants should be kept moist but not wet and soggy. Temperature can be the regular temperature of the household. And, of course, they need fresh air. The water used should be that which has been drawn a few days ahead from the tap or well water, but don't use water that has been standing in a plastic container.

INDEX

Edna Lewis was born in Freetown, Virginia, a farming community founded after the Civil War by freed slaves (among them her grandfather). For years she lived in New York, where she started her career at the famed Café Nicholson.

Ms. Lewis was the recipient of numerous awards, including the Grande Dame des Dames d'Escoffier International (1999). Together with Scott Peacock, she helped create the Society for the Revival and Preservation of Southern Food. She was also the author of *The Edna Lewis Cookbook, In Pursuit of Flavor,* and, with Scott Peacock, *The Gift of Southern Cooking.* She retired to Decatur, Georgia, where she died in February 2006.